Crossing Over

Getting to the Best Life Yet

Paul Scanlon

THOMAS NELSON
Since 1798

NASHVILLE   DALLAS   MEXICO CITY   RIO DE JANEIRO   BEIJING

Published in Nashville, Tennessee, by Thomas Nelson, Inc. www.thomasnelson.com

Nelson Books titles may be purchased in bulk for educational, business, fund-raising, or sales promotional use. For information, please e-mail SpecialMarkets@ThomasNelson.com.

All Scripture quotations, unless otherwise indicated, are taken from The New King James Version (NKJV®), copyright 1979, 1980, 1982, Thomas Nelson, Inc., Publishers. Other Scripture references are from the following sources: The Holy Bible, New International Version (NIV). Copyright ©1973, 1978, 1984, International Bible Society. Used by permission of Zondervan Bible Publishers. The Message (MSG), copyright ©1993. Used by permission of NavPress Publishing Group.

Library of Congress Cataloging-in-Publication Data

Scanlon, Paul, O.P.
  Crossing over : real change, real courage, real transformation / Paul Scanlon.
     p. cm.
  ISBN 978-1-59951-017-0
  1. Life change events—Religious aspects—Christianity.
  2. Adjustment (Psychology)—Religious aspects—Christianity.
  3. Bible. O.T. Joshua I-III—Criticism, interpretation, etc. I. Title.
  BV4908.5.S32 2007
  248.4—dc22

                                        2006033599

Printed in the United States of America
07 08 09 10 — 9 8 7 6 5 4 3

Contents

Introduction

"Crossing Over" is not about cosmetic change; it is about an extreme makeover.

Crossing over is about radical change; the prize is commensurate with the pain, and the problem is as big as the promise that follows it.

This book carries a message for all Christians even though it is directed at particular kinds of leaders and churches. There are many churches that may have had a great past but have no future without a radical transformation. To you I want to say: your day doesn't have to be over; your time needn't be past. The present struggles in your church may not be announcing the end of your ministry but the beginning of something new. Perhaps this book can help to explain and interpret your present season of life. As you read our story of "crossing over," it may help you make sense of where you and your church are today.

Every new move of God has a new language, a new vocabulary. In Isaiah 43:19, God declares, *I will do a new thing*. We must allow time to pass and room to grow before we start trying to over-define any "new thing" God may be doing. Even God doesn't attempt to name it; it's just a new thing. However, in the UK where I pastor, "crossing over" has become widely used to describe the journey thousands of churches must make. Without intending it, crossing over has become new vocabulary to interpret the otherwise confusing language of what's going on in many churches. Though all these churches are different, they all share common features of a crossing over scenario:

- A blessed past but a growing awareness that its future is not secure.
- Leaders who have deepening concerns for the future of their movement, business, church, or ministry, and who know that without radical change, it's over.
- Leaders for whom relevance to the lost has become a major issue, but who don't know how to move a comfortable church toward a less comfortable future.

- Increasing awareness of a need for a "wineskin" change, but confusion about what that actually looks like.

I want *Crossing Over* to be a kind of map, a signpost to help others navigate across their personal or corporate Jordan because, I promise you, when you start going against the status quo in your church, all hell may break loose!

God's Crash-Test Dummies

Crossing Over is my crash-test journal for all to read. I want to say to all my fellow pastors and leaders on the planet, "If I survived—so can you!" If my survival helps you to attempt what's in your heart, then my collisions, battles, and sleepless nights were all worth it. The deep-seated and, at times, gut-wrenching fear of attempting to escape a past that nobody wants to escape and the relief of finding the strength and support to enter your future can both be overwhelming. The apostle Paul said, *I bear in my body the marks*

(Galatians 6:17), or, in other words, "I'm a survivor; I'm a crash-test dummy; I'm living proof that no amount of resistance can stop you."

My desire is to become a crash-test dummy for other "crossing over" pilgrims. What I survived doesn't have to kill you, but in order for that to happen you must first know about the tests, crashes, and collisions that I walked away from.

I bear on my life the marks of our crossing over; they are in this book for all to see, and every one of them is saying the same thing: crossing over—the reinvention of the church—can be survived! More than that, I want every mark, scar, and blemish to read like the label on the leather couch I bought recently, which said: "This product is not faulty or damaged. All the markings, scarring, and discolorations on this product are normal and enhance its natural beauty."

One day you will be the "product" others will examine; maybe a fearful pastor will look to you for help and courage while attempting what is in his heart. Show him your label: "This person is not faulty or damaged. All the markings, scarring, and blemishes are normal and enhance the humanity and authenticity of a life lived in pursuit of the purpose of God."

Setting the Scene

Our church was about twenty-five years old and dying. We had certainly grown over the years from six people meeting together in a home to around 450 now regularly attending—a large church by UK standards. During this time we had also started eight other churches in our region by sending groups of fifty or more adults from our congregation into the neighboring towns and cities. We were a good church; some may even say a great church—the flagship church in our particular group of churches. We were a deeply committed family, loving and nurturing, holding regular evangelistic events and enjoying vibrant church services. Our building was virtually debt-free, we had money in the bank, and the people were generous givers.

Everything about our church seemed to be saying, "All is well," and there was nothing to be alarmed about. But in my heart alarm bells were ringing. The comfort, safety, and security that a church like ours enjoyed and offered was my greatest concern because it was our greatest enemy.

During this period of growing concern, I

began to look at my own church as a doctor would examine a patient. In a detached, clinical, and calculating way, I started to examine the body of our church for symptoms of the sickness I knew we had and feared could be terminal. It's not easy to attend your own church as a visitor or look at your own body or life's work objectively; but to survive, we must.

It's not easy to attend your own church as a visitor or look at your own body or life's work objectively; but to survive, we must.

I remember one particular Sunday morning so clearly. I was watching the church assemble and observing what I'd been a part of for years but had never seen: people entered the sanctuary, put down their belongings on or under chairs, and walked away to chat with each other. Car keys, house keys, purses, cell phones, and so on, were all left unguarded as we all just fellowshipped with each other. This scene became a statement about the condition of our church. That statement was simply, "We are not reaching the lost." We were so comfortable and so confident that strangers who might steal our stuff were not present that we did something in church we wouldn't dream of doing anywhere else in our daily lives. Our abandoned

valuables strewn on the floor were testament to the safety and comfort levels we had drifted into.

Now, years later, our floors are spotless and we guard our stuff because there are so many visitors present whom we don't know and cannot vouch for. I realized, as every senior pastor must, that our future church was among lost people, and unless we started reaching out to them, we had no future. The prospect of growing old while looking at the same few faces in church was scary—too scary to live with!

> *Our future church was among lost people, and unless we started reaching out to them, we had no future.*

In 1998, and several months into this season of asking, "What's wrong with our church?" my own sense of destiny and vision were forming strongly within me. I knew God had called me to build a church of thousands, and I also knew some in our present church would never embrace all the changes that would require. Our six hundred-seat building of nine years was already proving inadequate, and I knew in my heart that it could never facilitate my vision for thousands. I decided, together with my team, to build a new two thousand-seat building for the growth I knew would come if I was obedient to God. By early 1999 the earth movers were on site digging out the foundations when God so clearly spoke to me.

The new building was fifty yards across the parking lot from our present building. As I looked out of my office window at the foundations being dug, God said, "You are not building a new building; you are starting a new church." God emphasized to me that in twelve months, when the project was complete, we shouldn't just change our address. We should change our church. At that moment, I first heard the term "crossing over" in my spirit. God said to me, "In twelve months you will cross this church over into their promised land."

God said to me, "In twelve months you will cross this church over into their promised land."

I instantly recognized the terminology from Joshua 1—3, which details how Joshua "crossed the people over" the Jordan River into their promised land. Instantly I could see the bigger picture, the master plan that I hadn't yet seen but knew was there. To me the parking lot became the Jordan River we were to cross, the new two thousand-seat auditorium became Canaan, and our present building became the wilderness. All of this made me a kind of Joshua, and so I turned to his life for wisdom. In one year we would march into that new building, but more importantly, we would march into our future. I was to start a new church inside the old church, and that would be the church that would cross over with me.

The rest of this book is about that journey. It is not our personal story as much as it is a record of the principles and concepts we discovered along the way that will work anywhere. I warn you that this journey is not for the fainthearted; it will require great courage. Eight years and thousands of people later, I know I heard God. I wonder if deep in your heart, you know God is also calling you to your own crossing over. Whatever you do, don't stop now. Keep going, for the best is yet to come.

Chapter 1

Preparing to Cross Over

"Crossing over" can describe your journey from one level of life to another; your journey from one season to another; your journey from what was to what is. For me it describes the journey from being yesterday's church to becoming the church of today and tomorrow. It is a process that every living, growing, healthy ministry or church will go through at some point. Such "crossings" nearly always require major change, which can be unsettling at best and traumatic—even devastating—at worst. The opportunity to "cross

1

over" comes to every generation, and while it can be refused, it cannot be denied or avoided. Everything that wants to grow and have a relevant future has to change, and change is God's gift to humanity. "Crossing over" is my language for and description of the change which thousands of churches must embrace, or they will face extinction.

> *Everything that wants to grow and have a relevant future has to change, and change is God's gift to humanity. "Crossing over" is my language for and description of the change which thousands of churches must embrace, or they will face extinction.*

In this chapter, I want to share with you *six steps of preparation* for crossing over. These are fundamental to the success of what comes next, so don't be tempted to skim over this initial chapter. I know that preparation is the part of any process we least enjoy, but without it, whatever we do will not be a thing of quality. In the next chapter we will begin to explore the practical dynamics of crossing over in more detail.

Throughout this book we will draw widely from Joshua's experience of leading God's people, Israel, across the river Jordan, as recorded in the Book of Joshua 1—3. Their "crossing over" was the final act that closed the door on their slavery in Egypt and the forty years of wilderness wandering. So, for our illustrative purposes, the Jordan represents the final barrier that God wants you to cross over. Crossing over your "Jordan" will take you from a past you must leave and project you forward to take possession of the promise-filled future God has for you. It is what the real you instinctively wants; you want to break through, go up, press in, cross over, and possess.

> *It is what the real you instinctively wants; you want to break through, go up, press in, cross over, and possess.*

Crossing the Jordan therefore represents the transition between where you are now and where God wants you to be. It might be a *personal* crossing over to achieve your God-given destiny. Alternatively, it may be a *corporate* crossing over that is needed. As a church, business, or ministry, it may mean making radical changes to the culture and structure of your organization in order to cross over into the future you see.

Whether personal or corporate, crossing over will involve great upheaval and personal pain in your life. It will require a great deal of courage and the ability to hold firm to your

3

convictions. Crossing over will not be easy, and those who call for it will not be popular.

A "Crossing Over" Perspective

The principles which helped us to cross over our church successfully were discovered through our own experiences. They are rooted in our own painful reality. They come to you having been lived out in us, and for that reason, I am confident about their authenticity. At some point we must answer the challenge both history and destiny have put before us—the challenge God has led us to face. Every year, thousands of churches close, and while some should close, many do so because of a failure to reinvent themselves and cross over into their new day.

Although many would aspire to and appreciate the benefits of Canaan, few are willing to surrender and separate from past mentalities, practices, and relationships. Every gardener understands the difference between annual and perennial plants. Annuals come once and then die whereas perennials stay in the ground and regenerate every year. In life, and particularly church life, we fail to discern this same difference between what was good but must die, and what is still good and must stay. Crossing over is as much about discovering what we must leave behind as it is about embracing what we can keep.

Crossing over is as much about discovering what we must leave behind as it is about embracing what we can keep.

Six Stages of Preparation

During our journey, we identified six stages of preparation that are essential to crossing over. If you follow these six things, you will be left with no other option than to go forward because the first stage is so final that it immediately places you at the point of no return. So, if you are not yet prepared to follow through, stop here! Whatever you do, don't experiment and then abandon the process. Think through each stage carefully, and then take them in sequence. These are the stages:

- Separation
- Confirmation
- Courage
- Commitment
- Secrecy
- Favor in the city

1. Separation—"Moses is dead!"

Joshua 1:1 tells us of Moses' death. When God told Joshua that Moses was dead, it wasn't just *information,* it was also *separation.* Joshua already knew that Moses was dead, but initially he didn't realize that Moses' death was a physical separation requiring conceptual and generational separation too. For God's people to complete the next phase of their journey, there had to be a "separation"—a severing of the things of the past in order to grasp the future. Separation is always the first act of possession. If you really want to receive something new, you must let go of something old first. It is a life principle. Historically the church has not been good at letting go; we want to possess the new but still keep the old. Jesus said

> *Separation is always the first act of possession. If you really want to receive something new, you must let go of something old first. It is a life principle.*

6

that unless a kernel of wheat goes into the ground and dies, it cannot release a harvest (John 12:24). Something always has to die in order for the life within it to live.

The first thing we must do in order to cross over is separate ourselves from everything we cannot take forward with us. You can't have Joshua *and* keep Moses. You can't have the wilderness *and* Canaan. You can't always keep the people you have *and* reach the ones you want. Consider the "Moses mentalities" in your past. What things were valid parts of your yesterday but have no place in your tomorrow? Anything, from dead and irrelevant traditions to ministries, church departments, staff, and leaders, which either cannot or will not transition to the next level, must be separated. This is the hardest part—separating from people with whom you thought you would grow old.

If you attempt to change things, some people will not stick around; they won't go quietly, and they will probably take others with them. That's a sad truth, but it is pointless to hold on to people who don't want to go on the journey with you. People don't like change, and some actually have a vested interest in things not changing.

God wanted Joshua to understand he could not lead the people the way Moses had. God knew that most of the people had not grasped this fact, but Joshua, their new leader, must. They could no longer function under the old regime with its old wilderness mind-set, and neither can we. God did not want Joshua or the people to live under the shadow of Moses. His death announced a separation from the previous way of doing things that had worked for his generation but now needed to change. This is the challenge that faces us all if we are committed to crossing over and possessing all God has in store for us. Moses is dead! He was awesome in his time, but this isn't his time; it's yours and your generation's. You are the Joshuas of today.

2. Confirmation—"You are my choice."

The second stage of preparation was *confirmation*. After God established the *separation* from the old way of doing things through Moses' death, He confirmed Joshua's position as leader. God wanted Joshua to know that he was "the man" and could do anything. In preparation for crossing over, God has already identified those who are able to go forward and lead others. Somebody must step up and be the leader because nobody has been where you are going next. These leaders are the people who can *smell* Canaan already; they can *taste* it now, even *see* it, though they are not there yet. They are drunk with the promise of a new day and the possibility of another chance to enter their promised future.

God said to Joshua, *As I was with Moses, I will be with you. I will not leave you nor forsake you* (Joshua 1:5). With these words God confirmed Joshua's leadership. He gave Joshua the stamp of approval. God made it clear He was *with* Joshua—not less than He was with Moses, not almost as much as He was with Moses, but with Joshua *just like* He was with Moses. We must know that God is with us because there will be times in the transition period when it will feel like no one else is.

There were times in the early stages of our crossing over when I felt very alone as the senior leader. I knew that others were with me, but many of them would not find the courage or confidence to express it until much later. The willingness to stand alone for a season, if necessary, was an important discovery for me. You need to know what it is like to stick with Jesus and, if necessary, go on alone. Up to that point I thought my leadership had approval and support from those over and around me. To go forward without those approvals or endorsements was new

9

and frightening. However, staying where we were as a church was even more frightening to me. I was determined to reach our "promised land."

Some of you reading this are addicted to people's approval, especially people you respect and admire. But some of these good people—even inadvertently—will resist your progress down what seems to be a reckless path. You must know, deep down, that you have heard from God; He is with you, and if you will only keep moving, you will meet others who are also with you. God wants to confirm us in what we are doing, because, *No one who puts his hand to the plow and looks back is fit for service in the kingdom of God* (Luke 9:62 NIV). If all this sounds divisive to you, it is! Revelation both unites and divides, and the revelation of the future that you can't let go of will be no different.

Revelation both unites and divides, and the revelation of the future that you can't let go of will be no different.

3. Courage—"Be very courageous."

Be strong and of good courage . . . be strong and very courageous . . . do not be afraid nor be dismayed (Joshua 1:6-9). Why did God need to tell Joshua so many times? Because He knew how important courage would be to the success of Joshua's mission—and how destructive *discouragement* could be. Someone has said that discouragement is the leukemia of the soul. As leukemia attacks the life-giving power of blood, so discouragement tries to attack the life of our God-given passions.

Perhaps more believers have been taken out by discouragement than anything else. Courage is the greatest among many admirable virtues. Once courage is present, it acts like an anchor for all the rest. Commitment, wisdom, planning, and decision-making all come easier with courage. Joshua couldn't afford the luxury of fear and discouragement, and neither can we.

The level of anger, upset, and resistance from some people in my church was shocking. Those who resisted our reinvention most vigorously were pastors, elders, deacons, and department heads. They were my first introduction to what I call the "church mafia"! They were church bullies trying to intimidate and control a leadership set on a new direction—a direction which might well dispossess their positions. Don't get me wrong; these were good people, and many of them were our friends. But you must never let good people keep you out of your best life. They tried to intimidate me with the threat of removing financial support, reporting me to those who were over me, and even leaving the church and taking others with them. My wife and I came under huge personal attack, as did the few other leaders who had dared to align with us. We had many long, lonely, and discouraging days—days when it looked like they were right and we were wrong. But I would live every one of those miserable days again for what we have now.

Be strong and courageous! God is drawn to courage; He loves courage. Hebrews 11 lists the heroes of the faith. It is certainly not a list of people who were living a perfect life or, in some cases, a holy life. Rather, it is a list of courageous people, many of whom would not be welcome in most churches today—a prostitute, a murderer, a deceiver, and so on. I've met people with apparently perfect lives who lacked courage and people whose lives were far from perfect who had lots of courage. And I know which ones I'd rather have alongside me in a tough situation!

God is drawn to courage.

Whatever happened to courage in the church? Where are God's bravehearts?

4. Commitment—"We are with you."

God chose Joshua as Moses' successor; He affirmed him and set him apart as the next leader (see Deuteronomy 34:9; Joshua 1:1). Shortly after, the people came to Joshua and said, *All that you command us we will do, and wherever you send us we will go* (Joshua 1:16). God's *affirmation* of Joshua was followed by a *confirmation* in the hearts of the people. The people showed their commitment to Joshua by pledging to follow him across the Jordan.

Once some people realize that you have been willing to separate from the past and have the courage to keep going for the future, they will support you. What's in your heart is in other people's hearts too, but some need to see strength to find strength. It won't be everybody; it probably won't be the majority and almost never includes some you most want it to be. People don't commit to weakness or instability, they commit to strength and courage. Once you believe that God is with you and start to live like He is, you will draw support, courage, and commitment from others.

What's in your heart is in other people's hearts too, but some need to see strength to find strength.

13

Please understand, particularly the leaders who are reading this, people's support and encouragement *follow* your separation and courage. *You* have to move first, without even knowing if anyone will follow. That's why you are called a leader!

When our church crossed over, I had to decide that if only a handful of people came with me, I would still continue. I had to find the strength to appear to be a failure before I could succeed. In reality, hundreds stuck with me, but I didn't know that until I was way past the point of no return.

5. Secrecy—"Be careful who you tell."

Joshua recognized the need for secrecy. The first spying mission to the Promised Land ended in failure, costing millions their destiny. Joshua had been a key player in that event forty years earlier, and he had learned from his experiences in the wilderness. Imagine his frustration and resentment at having to call off entering the Promised Land because of the unbelief of others. I imagine that he must have said to himself, "If I get my chance, I will definitely do this a bit differently."

Moses had sent his spies out very publicly. They were all high-profile community leaders, and whatever they came back with would determine everyone else's response. Joshua, however, opted for secrecy, and it is easy to see why. The whole nation had waited with bated breath for Moses' spies to return with their report. Imagine the speculation that must have been going on while the spies were away. In the same way, there can be needless speculation in the church, if your plans to cross over your "Jordan" are aired prematurely. Joshua must have said to himself, "I will never make that mistake; I will tell no one until the time is right," and that is what he did. When the time came, he sent his spies over the Jordan into Jericho in secret. They were anonymous, it was a low-key operation, no one knew they had left, and they reported back privately to Joshua.

At the beginning of our crossing over, the first steps were made privately. Saying too much too soon would have created problems, started too many rumors, and caused too much instability. Announcements from the pulpit or unguarded conversations will not always win the commitment of the people; they can become nervous and uncertain about implied changes with what they've always been comfortable. You have to be able to keep a secret and work quietly, confidentially.

Such privacy, especially about the workings of the church, may be difficult for you.

It certainly was not easy for me because, historically, I had built close, covenant relationships based on openness and accountability. When I kept quiet, I felt like I was being deceitful. I had to get past that feeling, and you will, too.

I realize that secrecy and privacy are not the church's best strengths. Because of the community and openness in a fellowship of faith, people feel as if they can share anything they've heard. Therefore, sometimes the less we tell people, the better it is. The moment the wrong people have your information, it becomes subject to their contamination by uninvited and unwanted opinions. It is better to say nothing than to say something and then spend your time trying to play it down and explain it away. Secrecy was certainly a huge key to the success of Joshua's crossing over, and it will be for you too.

As your plan develops, choose carefully with whom you share information. Initially, only involve people who *see what you 'are*

Therefore, sometimes the less we tell people, the better it is. The moment the wrong people have your information, it becomes subject to their contamination by uninvited and unwanted opinions.

seeing—regardless of who they were under the previous administration. If you can do this, then when the time is right to reveal the plans for crossing over, you will already have developed a strong immunity against the negativity, criticism, and unbelief of others.

The bottom line is: Guard your heart; be careful whom you speak to and what you say. Don't allow yourself to be hijacked by the opinions of others. Don't talk openly about things you are not ready to disclose. Keep your own counsel.

6. Favor in the city—"Friends in low places."

God gave Joshua a way into the city of Jericho through Rahab the prostitute. Once the spies had entered the city, the king of Jericho somehow found out and went on a house-to-house search for them. Rahab risked her life and not only hid them but sent their pursuers away in the wrong direction. Then we read:

> Before the spies lay down for the night, she went up on the roof and said to them, "I know that the LORD has given this land to you and that a great fear of you has fallen on us, so that all who live in this country are melting in fear because of you. We have heard

how the Lord dried up the water of the Red Sea for you when you came out of Egypt, and what you did to Sihon and Og, the two kings of the Amorites east of the Jordan, whom you completely destroyed. When we heard of it, our hearts melted and everyone's courage failed because of you, for the Lord your God is God in heaven above and on the earth below. Now then, please swear to me by the Lord that you will show kindness to my family, because I have shown kindness to you. Give me a sure sign that you will spare the lives of my father and mother, my brothers and sisters, and all who belong to them, and that you will save us from death."

"Our lives for your lives!" the men assured her. "If you don't tell what we are doing, we will treat you kindly and faithfully when the Lord gives us the land."

So she let them down by a rope through the window, for the house she lived in was part of the city wall. Now she had said to them, "Go to the hills so the pursuers will not find you. Hide yourselves there three days until they return, and then go on your way" (Joshua 2:8-16 NIV).

To have *favor in the city*—in your own geographical area—is critical for churches who desire to cross over because the city is your future church. We must realize that most of the people who are yet to join our "church" aren't even saved! Your future church is among the thousands of people who don't yet know you exist. God gave Joshua a sign, showing him there were God-fearing people in the city of Jericho who were more willing to risk their lives to help him cross over into Canaan than some of his own people. God had unusual allies in the city. A woman known as Rahab the prostitute became Joshua's greatest helper. Not the governor, mayor, or city leaders, but a prostitute.

Your future church is among the thousands of people who don't yet know you exist.

Maybe we need to reverse our thinking about how we influence a city. Communities are changed from the grass roots up, not from the top down. We all need friends in low places to influence a community. Every politician understands this. If a politician can get the support of the grass roots of a country in sufficient numbers, he will win. You may think you need to curry favor with the rich, famous, and influential to win a city, and while that can help, it is always insufficient.

No doubt many in the city thought of Rahab as the dregs of society, yet this woman must have told the spies things they could never have otherwise known. She knew the word on the street better than anyone. She told them what the government of the city was saying; she told them what the word was on the political and military grapevine. Let's face it, she had probably slept with some of those in authority and knew all the stuff that even people in positions of authority didn't know. She told the spies what she knew, and the spies reported back to Joshua. That must have done something very affirming to his heart. Joshua must have felt that there was "favor in this city" and that God had given him allies in strategic places. What this does in a leader's heart is priceless.

Rahab represents the thousands of people who are open to God in our communities, but who don't feel that they would ever be welcome in a church. None of us in church life will ever meet our "Rahabs" as long as we try only to keep those already in the church happy and try to maintain our church's status quo. Rahab is on your side, but she won't come to you;

> *Rahab is on your side, but she won't come to you; you must go to her house, her streets, her world.*

you must go to her house, her streets, her world.

The deepest concern I had for our church was that we were not growing. We were not reaching lost people. Our church was twenty-five years old, with a weekly attendance of about four hundred people, and was successful by UK church standards. But we were dying a slow death that no one seemed to have noticed or be alarmed about. This describes thousands of churches, filled with good people who love God but have forgotten why they exist. I had forgotten why we existed. I was so busy servicing the needs of overfed and under-exercised Christians that I had stopped mobilizing them to address a lost world.

I knew what we needed to do but wasn't sure how to start. I needed an idea. That idea came in the form of a bus ministry. In April 1999, just a few months into our crossing over journey, someone handed me a book by Pastor Tommy Barnett called, *There's a Miracle in Your House*. In his book, Tommy explained how he had used a bus ministry to grow his church. Although the bus ministry was only mentioned in passing, the idea stuck with me. Within days we had found a mini-bus rental company and the following Sunday had a family of five ride our very first bus to church. The following week they brought others, until we were bringing hundreds of "Rahabs" to our Sunday services including some from the most deprived areas of the city.

Well, as you can imagine, not everyone in the church liked this and they began to line up to let me know just how much they didn't! The best thing for me, as mentioned in my introduction, was seeing the floor and chairs spotless on Sunday morning. People sat holding their stuff for fear that one of those "bus people"—as some called them—would steal their valuables. Suddenly our church wasn't safe anymore, and I had my sign of "favor in the city" from those grassroots people who by the hundreds were giving their lives to God.

Prior to 1999, despite our having been in the city for twenty-five years, virtually no one knew we existed. Now, just a few years later, we are known throughout the city as "the church that helps people"—the kind of people most churches would not welcome.

Consider these six stages of preparation carefully:

- Separation
- Confirmation
- Courage

- Commitment
- Secrecy
- Favor in the city

Think about these stages carefully as you prepare for your own crossing over journey, and in the next chapter we will look at six additional principles of crossing over, once again based on Joshua's example and experience.

Chapter 2

Crossing Over

After the preparation stage comes the time to step out and begin your journey into the future you see. The following principles were a great help to me, and I hope they will be to you.

For the children of Israel, crossing the Jordan was the pivotal moment in their journey from slavery in Egypt to freedom in Canaan, their land of promise. It was a moment that required a particular kind of leadership—Joshua leadership. The name Joshua means "savior," a name that is not without significance when we understand the true nature of crossing over and the life or death implications for our lives and churches.

Moses-style leadership can get you out of Egypt, but you are going to need a Joshua to get you into your Canaan. Joshua was a warrior, a soldier. He led Israel in all their wars and was built for a fight. Joshua leadership is "breakthrough" in nature; it is conquering and possessing. It is leadership that delivers and saves. Somewhere at the forefront of every barrier-breaking business, team, or church are leaders like this. They are built for the kill and born to dismantle the status quo that resists their future. Sadly, this kind of leadership appears to be lacking in many churches today. Too many churches are stuck in the past, and there they will stay without a Joshua to lead them out.

Joshua leadership is "breakthrough" in nature; it is conquering and possessing. It is leadership that delivers and saves.

Using Joshua's experience once again, let's examine six principles which will help us navigate some of the unique challenges crossing over presents us with. First, Joshua 3 (NIV) tells us how Joshua did it:

Early in the morning Joshua and all the Israelites set out from Shittim and went to the Jordan, where they camped before crossing over. After three days the officers went throughout the camp, giving orders to the people: "When you see the ark of the covenant of the LORD *your God, and the priests, who are Levites, carrying it, you are to move out from your positions and follow it. Then you will know which way to go, since you have never been this way before. But keep a distance of about a thousand yards between you and the ark; do not go near it."*

Joshua told the people, "Consecrate yourselves, for tomorrow the LORD *will do amazing things among you." Joshua said to the priests, "Take up the ark of the covenant and pass on ahead of the people." So they took it up and went ahead of them. And the* LORD *said to Joshua, "Today I will begin to exalt you in the eyes of all Israel, so they may know that I am with you as I was with Moses. Tell the priests who carry the ark of the covenant: 'When you reach the edge of the Jordan's waters, go and stand in the river.' "*

Joshua said to the Israelites, "Come here and listen to the words of the LORD *your God. This is how you will know that the living God is among you and that he will certainly drive out before you the Canaanites, Hittites, Hivites, Perizzites, Girgashites, Amorites and Jebusites. See, the ark of the covenant of the Lord of all the earth will go into the Jordan ahead of you. Now then, choose twelve men from the tribes of Israel, one from each tribe. And as soon as the priests who carry the ark of the LORD—the Lord of all the earth—set foot in the Jordan, its waters flowing downstream will be cut off and stand up in a heap."*

So when the people broke camp to cross the Jordan, the priests carrying the ark of the covenant went ahead of them. Now the Jordan is at flood stage all during harvest. Yet as soon as the priests who carried the ark reached the Jordan and their feet touched the water's edge, the water from upstream stopped flowing. It piled up in a heap a great distance away, at a town called Adam in the vicinity of Zarethan, while the water flowing down to the Sea of the Arabah (the Salt Sea) was completely cut off. So the people crossed over opposite Jericho. The priests who carried the ark of the covenant of the LORD stood firm on dry ground in the middle of the Jordan, while all Israel passed by until the whole nation had completed the crossing on dry ground.

Six Principles of Navigation

- Recognize that by crossing over you are "saving" the church.

28

- The ark is not as supernatural as the cloud because it's time to grow up.
- You are on your own for the first thousand yards.
- You will get cold feet!
- To enter a new flow, you must first break the old flow.
- Leaders must stand firm until everyone has crossed over.

1. Recognize that by crossing over you are "saving" the church.

At times as leaders, we become aware that our choices will ultimately make or break our churches. It is at those times that the true price and privilege of leadership come to bear on our lives. The awareness that our choices can affect people's spiritual journey and even compromise their progress, is the most sobering part of what we as leaders do. One day we will all stand before God and give an account of how we handled our lives. But from us as leaders, a double accounting will be required—first for ourselves and then for the way we handled the lives of the people we led.

Never before, in all my years of leadership prior to our church crossing over, had I felt the huge responsibility for people's lives and destinies as I did then. Paramedics save lives, fire fighters save lives, surgeons and soldiers all save lives, but pastors don't. I realized during the early months of our church crossing over that I was actually involved in saving people's lives. I don't think for a moment that the church understood I was a savior, but that didn't matter. What mattered was that I realized it. It was this awareness that my leadership was literally creating a new future for people that kept me going in the face of much adversity.

To every pastor reading this I want to say, you are a life saver! The choices you make, particularly during a generational transition for your church, will be life-and-death choices for you, the church, and the community. May the Joshua within you wake up!

You are a life saver! The choices you make, particularly during a generational transition for your church, will be life-and-death choices for you, the church, and the community.

2. The ark is not as supernatural as the cloud because it's time to grow up.

For forty years the children of Israel had been led by supernatural guidance. A cloud led them by day, and a pillar of fire led them at night. Whenever the cloud moved, they moved. They didn't need a map, a leader, or a plan; they just followed the cloud.

However, on the day they crossed over the river into Canaan, the cloud disappeared. Instead of looking up to the cloud overhead, they now had to look toward the ark carried by the priests. All this was part of God weaning the Israelites off their dependency on the cloud and teaching them to trust and follow the leadership of men—something with which they would struggle. It is one thing for a leader to step up and be God's "Joshua" in a situation, but it's quite another for people to follow that leadership. For people who have relied on guidance by "cloud" through prophecy, words, visions, and dreams, it is not easy to let go and follow godly leaders.

The ark, though sacred to every Hebrew, was still man-made and man-moved. The cloud, in contrast, was utterly supernatural— created, positioned, and moved by God.

Our church had its fair share of the "cloud" crowd—people whose sense of divine guidance was very personal, subjective, and sovereign. We had a culture of prophesying directly over people, which deepened the belief that God only leads in that manner. Some were regarded particularly as prophetic—which meant they heard from God more than most—and had an accuracy that made us dependent on them for final confirmation regarding our seemingly less clear sense of direction. Undoubtedly there was much good among all this, but the downside was a tendency to be super-spiritual and intense about God's guidance in our lives. We followed leadership, but only as much as they seemed to be following the cloud. We had an unhealthy dependence on the approval of certain prophetic leaders, which resulted in a reluctance to follow more "ordinary" leadership, such as a local church pastor.

All over the world God has and is raising men and women to lead His people into an awesome future. These new leaders are smart, sharp, streetwise, and acutely aware of what is and isn't relevant to the twenty-first century church.

All over the world God has and is raising men and women to lead His people into an awesome future. These new leaders are smart, sharp, streetwise, and acutely aware of what is and isn't relevant to the twenty-first century church. To the "cloud crowd" they may appear less spiritual and less supernatural, but without their down-to-earth, in-touch leadership, nobody is going over to Canaan. Nobody!

3. *You are on your own for the first thousand yards.*

> *When you see the ark of the covenant of the L*ORD *your God, and the priests, who are Levites, carrying it, you are to move out from your positions and follow it. Then you will know which way to go, since you have never been this way before. But keep a distance of about a thousand yards between you and the ark; do not go near it"* (Joshua 3:3-4 NIV).

God instructed the people of Israel to keep a distance of a thousand yards between them and the ark of the covenant when they crossed over the river Jordan. They were not to get too near it. This illustrates something that I call "The Leadership Gap."

In leadership there is always a gap between the first person stepping out and the first person following. We cannot break through as a crowd; someone always has to go first, and this is never more true than when the future is unknown territory. There is a loneliness in leadership that is hard to explain and hard to bear. As leaders, even though we have people who are close

> *As leaders, even though we have people who are close to us, there is always a degree to which we are alone in spearheading the future.*

to us, there is always a degree to which we are alone in spearheading the future.

You are on your own for the first thousand yards—in other words, by the time the rest of the people get to where the leaders are, the breakthrough has already happened. The leaders had to step into the Jordan first, before anything happened. The majority of people who are following will never see what the leaders saw, feel what they felt, struggle with what they struggled with, or need the same faith they needed. Leaders are like arrowheads. Everything that comes after them will never have to penetrate the same level of resistance in order to break through.

This gap, this delay between stepping out and others following, is the first thousand yards we must do alone. If you are a leader reading this, I pray that you will not lose heart during this gap. Keep moving ahead, and I promise you others will join you soon.

4. You will get cold feet!

God instructed the priests carrying the ark of the covenant to enter the Jordan before all the people. He said, *When you have come to the edge of the water . . . you shall stand in the Jordan* (Joshua 3:8). They had to go and stand still in the river while apparently nothing was happening. In other words, the first people getting cold feet were—you guessed it—the leaders!

Church leaders, cold feet are a normal part of your life and calling. For the sake of God's people we will spend our lives out in front with cold feet. It doesn't mean that you are a doubter or an unbeliever, it just means that you are the first to initiate things with no guarantee of success! By the time others reach where you are, the water that looked like it wouldn't budge will have parted and their feet will be dry. To experience cold feet and keep going anyway, because you know there is nothing to go back for, is your gift of leadership to all who follow.

I had many cold feet moments as our church crossed over. Every decision I made to break with the past—the known and familiar—was a "did I do the right thing, will anybody follow me, will God bless this?" moment. If you have cold feet about going forward, it's not a sign to go back; it's a constant reminder that you are a leader.

> *If you have cold feet about going forward, it's not a sign to go back; it's a constant reminder that you are a leader.*

35

5. To enter a new flow you must first break the old flow.

It would seem that whenever we want to start something new, we must first break the momentum of the old. Joshua 3:13 reads, *"And it shall come to pass, as soon as the soles of the feet of the priests who bear the ark of the LORD . . . shall rest in the waters of the Jordan, that the waters of the Jordan shall be cut off . . . and they shall stand as a heap."* God had often spoken of Canaan as a land "flowing with milk and honey." This was the language of plenty, a picture of prosperity and provision in abundance. However, between the people and that new flow of abundance was the flowing Jordan that had to be crossed over. And to enter that new flow, the priests had to step into the existing flow of the swollen Jordan River.

This became a picture of what I had to do to access our future. Our church style and culture were not working, and they were keeping us out of our promised land—a land which was so close some of us could see it. Breaking into a fast-flowing river of any kind can be dangerous, but none more so than the river of dead traditions, ancient legalisms, and the many forms of control that flow in many churches. I was going to have to step into the swollen flow.

Moses never had to step into the water when he crossed the Red Sea; he just raised his rod and it parted in front of him. Joshua's generation of leaders, however, had to stand firm in the water, while apparently nothing was happening, and their miracle of the river's flow started upstream, well out of sight (Joshua 3:15–16). In other words, these waters didn't part, they dried up somewhere out of sight. This thought helped me greatly during our crossing over because more often than not, when I stepped into what wasn't working and tried to stop it, I ended up battling the current and seemingly making no difference. Only later in the process of crossing over did I realize that a parting of the waters was not what our church needed. We needed those who were unwilling to embrace the future, the protectors of the "old flow," to be cut off from having any further negative influence on our new flow. So I began a process of removing and repositioning people in leadership, cutting off their abilities to continue sending the wrong messages downstream into our children's futures.

Crossing over your Jordan barrier will mean you, as the leader, having to wade into situations and address things that don't appear to be a problem. We must reach a little upstream and deal with the root causes of the effects that keep coming downstream. Eventually I realized that the few things still trickling through our church from the past were not revived flows but only what was left in the pipe! Knowing we had dealt with things upstream, as it were, by confronting directly those people who were still generating the old flow, helped me to stay calm in the knowledge that the miracle of crossing over, though imperceptible to most, had already begun somewhere upstream.

6. *Leaders must stand firm until everyone has crossed over.*

> Then the priests who bore the ark of the covenant of the LORD stood firm on dry ground in the midst of the Jordan; and all Israel crossed over on dry ground, until all the people had crossed completely over the Jordan (Joshua 3:17).

Lastly, leaders must keep standing against the "old flow" until everyone who wants to has crossed over. The leaders are the ones who must hold firm to the vision until everyone is on "dry ground."

The strong currents from parts of our twenty-five year history had to be stopped.

Our leadership team had to stand firm. It took about two years, but we eventually broke that flow. This taught us that not everyone will be ready to enter a new season at the same time. So, while I am not advocating we wait forever for all the stragglers to cross, I am suggesting that we leave the door ajar so late adopters of the new thing God is doing can still join in.

In any move of God there are complex reasons why some people respond faster than others. Not everyone who is slow to "buy in" is necessarily resistant, rebellious, or awkward—and if we treat them as such, we may lose people we could have kept. As long as those priests stood in that dry river bed, everybody could be assured that the opportunity to cross over had not yet expired. It is important, especially during times of significant transition, that we lead in a way which waits for as many as possible to journey with us.

Not everyone who is slow to "buy in" is necessarily resistant, rebellious, or awkward—and if we treat them as such, we may lose people we could have kept.

In more recent years, "everybody who wants to cross over" has come to include thousands of leaders across the world whom I also feel a responsibility to help. This sense of call and responsibility to help other leaders and churches cross over has deepened to the point where I have now embraced it as a fundamental part of my life's calling.

I remember so clearly a conversation with a pastor about our crossing over during which he felt compelled to help me to calm down. He advised me to "move on and stop going on about it" because we had already crossed over and if I kept talking about it and about the bad old days, people would think I was dwelling on hurt feelings. I will never forget my response to his statement. I looked him straight in the eye and kind of blurted out from my spirit, "Yes, but thousands haven't, and I must help them!" To this day I feel that although our church has crossed over, I am still standing in that dry river bed because I know others are coming; many others are coming, and maybe you are one of them. They will need a guide to help them across, and I have volunteered my life to be a guide for those pilgrims to follow.

The Stones of Remembrance

God commanded Israel to take twelve stones out of the Jordan and set them on the bank as a monument to remind them of their crossing (Joshua 4:8–9). The stones would trigger future generations to ask about their forefathers' crossing over experience.

We in the local church must place some kind of marker posts into our church history. It's not nostalgia or a "good old days" thing; it's about keeping alive the memory of where we came from and what it cost some of us. When a new person joins our church, they have no idea about our crossing over season. But it is important that they know what some of us fought and suffered for in order to truly celebrate the freedoms we now enjoy. I didn't live through World War II. I didn't fight in it and don't know anyone who did. However I am deeply grateful to those who did go to war, because now, three generations later, I and millions of others are enjoying the freedoms they died for. While I never want to sit around in my old age telling my crossing over "war" stories to bored-looking teenagers, I do want them to remember, honor, and protect the freedoms we fought for. Our church must never ever go

> *While I never want to sit around in my old age telling my crossing over "war" stories to bored-looking teenagers, I do want them to remember, honor, and protect the freedoms we fought for.*

back to being the church we were, and I have placed my stones of remembrance all around our church and my ministry. This book is one of them.

We thank God that we survived our crossing over journey. The "old flow" has been broken, and we now shout to everybody who is still stuck on the other bank, "Come on over; it gets better from here."

Chapter 3

Delivered from People Possession

I have described what I mean by "crossing over" in the context of this book. Because you learned the six crucial stages of preparation and the six principles of navigation, you are now aware of the great responsibility which falls upon leadership. In the next two chapters, I want to discuss the qualities of the "crossing over leader." These convictions are based on my own experience of our church crossing over. I have tried to ensure my observations are objective and that others will relate to them.

Personally, I am a strong-willed, focused, determined person. I don't look for confrontation, but I've never avoided it when necessary, particularly when our future is at stake. We are all wired differently, and because there is no way to transition a church into a future that everybody will want, a degree of confrontation is inevitable. In fact, it is an inevitable consequence of reinventing anything. As leaders, we therefore have to settle a fundamental issue: we cannot allow things to slide or remain unaddressed simply because we don't want to deal with them. We cannot hold everyone else's future to ransom because of our personal limitations and fears. If you have to, do it scared. But do it! The fear of man is a snare, and some people can be scary.

We cannot hold everyone else's future to ransom because of our personal limitations and fears. If you have to, do it scared. But do it!

I want to help you with this fear of people. During the apostle Paul's trial before King Agrippa, he recounted some of the details about his Damascus road conversion experience:

On one of these journeys I was going to Damascus with the authority and commission of the chief priests. About noon, O king, as I was on the road, I saw a light from heaven, brighter than the sun, blazing around me and my companions. We all fell to the ground, and I heard a voice saying to me in Aramaic, "Saul, Saul, why do you persecute me? It is hard for you to kick against the goads."

Then I asked, "Who are you, Lord?"

"I am Jesus, whom you are persecuting," the Lord replied. "Now get up and stand on your feet. I have appeared to you to appoint you as a servant and as a witness of what you have seen of me and what I will show you. **I will rescue you from your own people and from the Gentiles. I am sending you to them to open their eyes** and turn them from darkness to light, and from the power of Satan to God, so that they may receive forgiveness of sins and a place among those who are sanctified by faith in me" (Acts 26:12–18 NIV, emphasis added).

I want you to notice one thing in particular that God said to him: *I will rescue you from your own people and from the Gentiles. I am sending you to them.* The King James Version translates this, *I will deliver you from the people to whom I will send you.*

Before we can help people as their leaders, we must first be delivered *from* the people. To be delivered from people means to be free of their control, intimidation, and manipulation. To be delivered from people means being able to hear from God, without having a "what will people think" mentality.

> *Before we can help people as their leaders, we must first be delivered from the people.*

During our crossing over, I remember so clearly how at various times, while discussing unpopular initiatives we were about to implement, people who were not even present still controlled the outcome. Certain names would always come up with a "what will they think?" question attached to them. Sometimes our planned course would be softened, altered, or even postponed until we could negotiate a way around the "church mafia." I remember coming into the church office one day, only to be greeted—yet again—by the news that a certain elder's wife had phoned to "bring correction" to my two newest, young staff members. She felt they had done a poor job on the church's weekly bulletin. This older woman, whom we all knew was totally against our crossing over, had so intimidated these two girls that they literally lived in fear of her. After weeks of this, I arranged a meeting between this lady and my two young future leaders. I had previously confronted this lady on several occasions about her attitude, but she was now quietly contacting and contaminating the next generation in an effort to intimidate them into doing things her way. These two girls were about to have their first taste of being delivered from people possession.

With some reluctance they went to the older lady's home for the meeting. By the time they arrived she had called her husband home to intimidate the girls doubly. My instruction to them had been, "Whatever you do, tell her exactly what you think and feel. Don't be intimidated, and don't hold back. Be sure she understands that her interference is both damaging and undermining you." And they did! They returned to the church office like two young Daniels just delivered from the lions' den and ready to take on the world!

Both those young women, then in their early twenties, are now part of our senior staff. One is our Worship Pastor, and the other is my daughter Charlotte, who now has a worldwide ministry of her own. If we don't break people's possession of our lives, it will

If we don't break people's possession of our lives, it will terrorize our children and our children's children.

terrorize our children and our children's children. That's how vital this principle is.

Some of you are in the middle of a similar situation today. You are living under the intimidation and control of people whom you may have once looked up to. That historic respect makes it even more difficult to deal with their resistance to a future they won't embrace. We are not ready to lead or serve people until we have uncoupled our souls from their control. If people possess us, own us, or manipulate us, we will always serve them before we serve God.

Later in Paul's life he wrote to the church at Corinth, *Though I am free and belong to no man, I make myself a slave to everyone, to win as many as possible* (1 Corinthians 9:19 NIV). This statement is an insight into what God began doing in him, back on the road to Damascus. He belonged to no man, which enabled him to be a voluntary slave to all men. Paul had come to realize that no one owned or controlled

Only when you are truly delivered from people, can God use you to reach people effectively.

him, and once that was established in his life, he became a lifelong servant of others. Only when you are truly delivered from people, can God use you to reach people effectively.

Jesus Refused to be Controlled by People

John tells us, *But Jesus did not commit Himself to them, because He knew all men, and had no need that anyone should testify of man, for He knew what was in a man* (John 2:24–25). Jesus had decided early on in His ministry that endorsement from people was a luxury He could not afford. He entrusted Himself to no man and needed no one's endorsement. Whether it was His enemies, like the Pharisees, or His family and loved ones, who also tried to control Him, He refused to entrust Himself to anyone who may have been capable of hijacking His destiny.

Imagine how devastated Jesus would have been if He had entrusted Himself to Peter, who had pledged undying love to Him but then three times denied ever knowing Him. Even those closest to you, especially those, must never be allowed to occupy a place of trust which leaves you looking to them for something which can only come from God. I love people as all true leaders do, but I must never give to people a level of trust that only belongs to God. That fundamental miscalculation opens the door to a life of overdependence on people which can only bring self-inflicted disappointment.

Like Jesus, the apostle Paul ended his life virtually alone. He writes to Timothy saying, *At my first defense no one stood with me . . . but the Lord stood with me and strengthened me* (2 Timothy 4:16–17). Paul had something that he never gave to a person. He drew strength from the Lord when everyone else deserted him. The only way we can continue our call and purpose when people desert us is by living free from people possession of our hearts and souls.

Pastor, leader, follower, are you people-possessed or people-controlled? If so, you will never set foot anywhere they don't want you to go. Begin today to uncouple yourself from ties that bind you to a past you know you must leave. You must be free, for yourself and for all who look toward your life for leadership. *You must be free from people to lead people.*

Chapter 4

Tamar Churches and Onan Leaders

I want to give you an example of what was happening in our church during crossing over. You may recognize this "type." Sometimes reading about Bible characters can be like reading about your own life. It's as if people in another time have already lived the script of your life and left footsteps to lead you to a possible outcome you hadn't seen or anticipated. The story of Onan and Tamar became that to me and our church.

If you are not familiar with the story of Onan and Tamar, please take a few minutes to read Genesis 38 now—it will greatly enrich your understanding of what follows. For those of you familiar with the story, let me take you to some verses at the crux of this unfolding episode:

> *And Judah said to Onan "Go in to your brother's wife and marry her, and raise up an heir to your brother." But Onan knew that the heir would not be his; and it came to pass, when he went in to his brother's wife, that he emitted on the ground, lest he should give an heir to his brother. And the thing which he did displeased the LORD; therefore, He killed him also"* (Genesis 38:8–10).

Onan Leaders

It fell to Onan to step in and ensure the continuation of Er, his dead brother's family lineage. Tamar was Er's widow, and she had been left childless by his sudden death. Whenever Onan slept with Tamar, he deliberately spilled his semen on the ground to avoid producing offspring for his brother. Onan's deceit and selfishness was more than God could bear, so He killed Onan. The utter pretense of his appearing to be doing the right thing but then doing the opposite, left Tamar in an impossible situation.

Here's how I interpreted Tamar and Onan into my crossing over experience. Tamar represented me and everyone like me in our church who was desperate to conceive and give birth to God's future. Onan represented each leader in our church who, while publicly appearing to be doing all the right things, was actually undoing all the right things.

This story of Onan and Tamar helped me to interpret what was going on in our church and many other churches across the world. The realization that some of our most senior leaders would not "seed" the next generation for fear of losing their own power base was shocking.

The realization that some of our most senior leaders would not "seed" the next generation for fear of losing their own power base was shocking.

Despite God placing the responsibility on Onan to help his brother's line continue on the earth, he didn't. Onan didn't want the responsibility of other mouths to feed, and more importantly, more people with whom he would have to divide his own wealth and possessions as he grew older. Onan spilled his seed to protect his own future; he cared more about himself than his dead brother's name or his bereaved, childless sister-in-law. Onan was obnoxious to God, because rather than openly refusing to help, he continued the appearance of helping to gain public approval but privately refused to endorse Tamar. When Onan deliberately spilt his semen on the ground, he was deliberately refusing to seed the next generation of his brother's line.

I had many Onan-type leaders prior to our church crossing over. Leaders who, while clinging to position and publicly appearing honorable, were behind-the-scenes seed spillers, refusing to fertilize those they knew were a threat to their future.

Onan leaders control fertility; they represent leadership which becomes unwilling to empower and release the next generation to its destiny. It's not that they don't have seed; they just don't release it into certain people whom they perceive as a threat to their own security. Onan leaders have the power, authority, position, and resources to help others into their calling but

> *Onan leaders control fertility; they represent leadership which becomes unwilling to empower and release the next generation to its destiny.*

develop a wasteful, seed-spilling habit, and God hates it.

An Onan spirit refuses to empower what it can't control, while clinging to its own power and position.

Tamar People

Tamar people were all those in our church who were so open, and even desperate, to conceive the new church we were becoming. Tamar can represent large numbers of people inside a dying church who refuse to die with it, and who, if they remain abandoned by Onan leaders, will go in pursuit of seed. That's exactly what Tamar did. She pretended to be a prostitute in order to trick her father-in-law, Judah, into sleeping with her and hopefully impregnating her (Genesis 38:15–30).

Tamar people will do anything and go anywhere to be a part of what God is doing. Every Sunday morning during our crossing over, I would stand up to preach, deliberately trying to sow the seeds of our future into the hearts of our church. All around the room were Onans, sitting with folded arms and frowning with disapproval. Every week I stood to minister became more and more difficult. I wasn't only battling Onan leaders in the room—some of whom were the elders sitting on the platform behind me—but I was also doing battle with all the behind-the-scenes confrontations from various delegations who came to see me during the week.

But I persevered, and slowly I was surrounded by more and more Tamars, who were catching the seed others were spilling. The more I preached about the church I knew we must become, the more the Tamars became pregnant. Within weeks I had lots of little "Zerahs" and "Perezes"—the twin boys Tamar eventually gave birth to—running around the church! Their names meant "breakout" and "brightness," and things beyond my control began to happen as these twins carrying our new breed DNA got loose in the church (Genesis 38:27–30).

Every time I wanted to deny responsibility for the upset these "terrible twins" were causing in the church, it was as if the people produced my seal and staff—just like Tamar did to Judah—to prove it was my seed (Genesis 38:25–26). People were quoting my messages to justify their new initiatives and confronting the Onans with my preaching. They knew the Onans still disapproved of the

Tamars' newfound fruitfulness. It was war between the house of Onan and the house of Tamar.

In church one Sunday morning, I remember being worn out by all the conflict and wondering where it would all end. Suddenly, I felt as if the Holy Spirit drew back a veil and opened my eyes, just like He did to Elisha's servant who saw the heavenly chariots of fire (2 Kings 6:17). As I looked out across the sea of hands raised in worship, I saw in the Spirit that many of the raised hands bore scarlet threads. These were people who had been "tagged" by God, who, like a midwife, had been helping these Tamars deliver our future church (Genesis 38:28). It was only then that I realized more were for me than were against me and that there could never be any going back.

God saw something so right in Tamar's heart that He blessed her and ultimately included her in Christ's faith genealogy (Matthew 1:3). Is your church a Tamar stuck under an Onan leadership? Are you getting older and remaining barren?

Churches must grow and produce leaders and followers for the future. Remaining under an Onan leadership is an impossible situation; it is wrong and abusive, but it is where millions of God's people live every day. I have no time for Onan. I have met him, suffered under him, wrestled with him, and prevailed over him, and so must you. It is time for Tamars everywhere to stand up and come out.

It is time for Tamars everywhere to stand up and come out.

To every Onan leader I say, let God's people go.

Don't make us choose, because we will choose life and we will leave you by our millions; we will leave you. Onan, we are not your problem, and we are not your enemy. We are Tamar, who came to your house for help, but you mishandled us, abused us, and robbed us of children.

At the heart of crossing over is the war between Onan leaders and Tamar people. The war is caused by those who will not relinquish their control and continue to resist any who threaten their status, position, and power. I had to include and record this stage of our journey for Tamar's sake and for Onan's warning. So, Tamar, wherever you are, don't die barren! The next generation depends on you, and I give you this book as my seal and staff, my ownership of responsibility to help you to conceive.

Chapter 5

What Kind of Church *Don't* You Want?

Early on I realized that I would not get another opportunity in my lifetime to cross the church over. Our church was twenty-five years old, was quite set in its ways, and had a culture that was introverted, safe, and exclusive. As the enormity of the opportunity dawned on me, I remember so clearly God asking me, "What kind of church *don't* you want?" That was an easier question for me to answer than, "What kind of church *do* I

His question helped me to look closely at what I didn't like about our church, and the things I didn't like soon became a small but radical list of things I knew would not easily die.

want?" His question helped me to look closely at what I didn't like about our church, and the things I didn't like soon became a small but radical list of things I knew would not easily die.

During this time of asking myself what was wrong with our church, I decided to spend several months traveling throughout the UK, asking the same question about many of the churches in our country. Many other churches like ours had enjoyed a few good years of blessing and growth during the Charismatic Renewal in the early 1970s. The overwhelming sense across the nation by the late 1990s, however, was that the majority of these churches were no longer growing, and the maintenance of the resulting apostolic networks, new church groups, and the older Pentecostal denominations had become the order of the day.

I want to share with you some of the things I observed in that period, followed by my interpretation of what I saw and, most importantly, my personal commitment to build what I called a "new breed" church. You may find my observations and conclusions beneficial to your business, movement, church, or ministry crossing over attempt.

Observation 1:

Every church service I visited started late with virtually no one there on time. During the first ten minutes the rest dribbled into the meeting, looking as if they didn't want to be there.

- *My Interpretation:* The church has lost their excitement about being together.
- *My Commitment:* I will build a church where services are so dynamic that no one will want to miss a moment. I will also build a culture of excellence, which starts with the basics of punctuality and reliability.

Observation 2:

Most churches I visited had passionless worship.

- *My Interpretation:* Worship has been reduced to the few songs dutifully sung prior to the preaching; the church is on autopilot.
- *My Commitment:* I will build a worshipping church, whose God-filled worship will be awesome and life-changing.

Observation 3:

People were generally nonresponsive and "dead," especially during the preached Word.

- *My Interpretation:* People are not excited about church. They are *attending* church instead of *being* the church. People are too "proper" in church and simply don't know how to, or even if it is OK to, respond to the Word of God. Also, most pastors do not communicate in a way that inspires a vocal response.
- *My Commitment:* I will build a church that is exciting to be in, that is not dominated by a reserved mind-

set, and where people are taught and shown how to respond appropriately in worship and to the Word.

Observation 4:

Old people were in charge of almost everything.

- *My Interpretation:* The next generation is not being released and empowered.
- *My Commitment:* I will empower the youth of our church to grow a younger church and build a young leadership team.

Observation 5:

Church buildings were generally in a very poor condition.

- *My Interpretation:* Excellence is missing in the church.

- *My Commitment:* We will build with excellence in all we do.

Observation 6:

There was little fun or laughter in the church.

- *My Interpretation:* The church is not comfortable with fun and humor in its corporate context. Many leaders lack personality, seem overly religious, and may have the wrong understanding of reverence.
- *My Commitment:* I will ensure that our collective church experience is fun, which means I must be a fun person. Laughter and joy must be at the core of our homes and church life.

Observation 7:

Weird, flaky stuff was allowed during services, such as testimonies about peculiar personal experiences without a strong faith base; weird public contributions and manifestations not supported by Scripture; totally inappropriate use of the gifts of the Spirit; mystical people saying mystical things that had no basis in the Christian faith or church history. Rather than outward signs of the Spirit's indwelling, these were mysterious, unscriptural occurrences that would be totally foreign and confusing to new believers.

- *My Interpretation:* The church has become a private "bless me" club, which has ceased reaching or being relevant to the lost. Leaders are not leading; they are as much if not more to blame for what they allow to happen.
- *My Commitment:* I will outlaw all weird and flaky things in our public services and make the services "lost friendly." I will rethink the practice of the gifts of the Spirit, ask for God's wisdom on this, and carefully guide believers about appropriate manifestations of the Spirit's indwelling.

Observation 8:

Powerless, irrelevant, long, and boring preaching dominated the services.

- *My Interpretation:* Many who are preaching are not called, gifted, or anointed to do so, and they are completely out of touch with what ordinary people need to hear. There is a famine of quality communicators in the church.
- *My Commitment:* I will work on my communication skills, stay in touch with what people need, and raise up other quality communicators.

Observation 9:

Many churches had long-winded teachings on giving prior to every offering.

- *My Interpretation:* People need too much encouraging and inspiring to give because many are essentially reluctant to do so.

• *My Commitment:* I will build a generous, giving church that gives because they see the dream and want to be a part of it.

Observation 10:

Very little vision was communicated publicly to the church.

• *My Interpretation:* There is a famine of visionary leaders, and God's people are dying because of a lack of vision.
• *My Commitment:* I will be a visionary leader who makes our vision plain, communicates it well, and raises others to do the same.

Observation 11:

Church leadership was primarily male.

• *My Interpretation:* Women are not being welcomed or empowered into leadership.

- *My Commitment:* I will empower women into leadership, especially the younger generation.

Observation 12:

Most churches were not growing, despite much prayer, prophecy, evangelism, and tears shed for the lost.

- *My Interpretation:* Churches are not actually reaching the lost. Prayer, prophecy, and tears don't replace bringing people to church.
- *My Commitment:* I will build a soul-winning, lost-bringing church. I will outlaw "virtual reality" evangelism; that is, we will not do anything which deceives people into thinking they are reaching the lost when in practice, they are personally reaching no one. We will refuse to weep over anything we won't do something practical about.

What I saw saddened me and helped me answer God's question, "What kind of church *don't* you want?" However, these twelve observations were just the most significant concerns I identified from a much longer list which included observations about:

- Length of services
- Dress codes
- Fashion
- Serving
- Décor
- Personal hygicnc
- Physical contact
- Jargon
- Time
- Administration
- Public announcements
- Stewards and greeters
- Sound engineers
- Musicians
- Hospitality
- Honorariums and generosity
- . . . and so on!

Among my comprehensive list of observations were many overlaps and repeats, all of which seemed to be pointing to the same few things. Together with a few others in my leadership team, we spent a day condensing all these concerns to what became three final concerns. These three became the ultimate expression of what was missing in so many churches. They also formed the beginning of what would become the new DNA of our crossed over church and my life's work. These three finalists were what, in my opinion, the church had ceased to be:

1. God-Centered
2. Purpose-Driven
3. People-Empowering

These three missing jewels from the church's crown became the three core strands in the formation of our new church DNA and the three primary values that would guide us in all we did in the future.

I had my answer to God's question and saw with absolute clarity that the church had lost her center, forgotten her purpose, and become controlling of her people. My life's work was unfolding before me. I must build a God-centered, purpose-

70

driven, people-empowering church. I must
not be people-centered, people-driven, or
people-controlled. I must not be movement-
centered, movement-driven, or movement-
controlled. I must never again be fear-
centered, fear-driven, or fear-controlled.

Of course, it is one thing to describe what
you don't like about the church and completely another to build what you do like. The
implementation was far more difficult than
the initial consultation process. But I began a
two-year process of removing all competing
centers, doing away with all alternatives to
purpose, and, above all, removing all who
would not lay down their people-controlling
leadership styles. I was shocked, saddened,
and angry at the extent to which we had
drifted off center, lost our sense of purpose,
and held people back. Nevertheless, I had my
answers to God's question and my future
work cut out for me.

The Church I See

It's not enough to want Canaan—we must
also know what was so bad about Egypt and

the wilderness. I have seen many leaders attempt "extreme church makeovers" who don't seem to have thought much about anything except the "extreme" part. They bulldoze the house and only then wonder about what should replace it! There's a process here: we must know what's wrong in order to do what's right. And both need consideration.

At the time of this writing, eight years after that DNA-discovering moment, our church has blossomed and morphed into a new creature. We have become the opposite of everything I hated about the state of other churches in our country. Now, thousands of people later, it's a joy to lead what I've since described as "The Church I See." "The Church I See" has become our vision statement. It is a further developed and filled-out expression of our new DNA and the practical outworking of our continued commitment to become the kind of people we must be for the sake of our children's future.

This description of "The Church I See" is mounted on the wall of our foyer for all to see, and hopefully it is in the hearts and actions of our people.

The Church I See . . .

THE CHURCH I SEE is God-centered, purpose-driven, and people-empowering.

THE CHURCH I SEE is exciting and full of life. It is a church that is both numerically large and spiritually deep.

THE CHURCH I SEE is non-religious, naturally supernatural, and incredibly fun to be in. It's a church of renowned character and integrity. A church whose number one priority is to glorify God and bring His wonderful life to a lost world.

THE CHURCH I SEE is attractive, confident, victorious, and overcoming. It is a church whose powerful proclamation and awesome worship are broadcast to the nations by every modern means possible.

THE CHURCH I SEE equips, enables, and releases ordinary people to live extraordinary lives.

THE CHURCH I SEE is a deeply committed, loving, caring family amongst whom the lonely and the broken find new hope and belonging.

THE CHURCH I SEE could well be this church, the Abundant Life Church, Bradford.

What kind of church *don't* you want? Describe it in all its breathtaking ugliness; see it from the unchurched point of view; understand how utterly resistible it is to a lost world. Then, paint a new picture with the new colors of the church you see. Finally, give yourself to building that amazing, irresistible church against which the gates of hell cannot possibly prevail.

Chapter 6

They Devoted
Themselves

I had a defining moment during this period of
our crossing over when I met an ex-Baptist
pastor who, after twenty years in ministry,
had resigned and was now a barkeeper. He
told me what had led him to this radical
change was twenty years of soul-destroying
ministry that put him and his wife on pre-
scription medication. He described a church
where he felt completely responsible to persuade people to get involved, but they
refused. He became worn out from the huge
effort required to convince, persuade,

remind, and sometimes beg people to get behind his vision, but they wouldn't.

I asked him what he enjoyed about being a barkeeper, and his reply hit me like a hammer. He said, "I love this job because my drinkers are devoted all by themselves." He explained how he never had to persuade or remind his customers to come back. He never had to call his absent drinkers to assure them they were missed, nor did he have to inspire them to part with their money. Finally, he said, "my drinkers come early and stay late, but in twenty years of ministry, the church did neither."

Wow! What an example of everything I had privately been thinking regarding the kind of church I wanted to build. This older man was a picture of my future unless I changed the culture of our church to one where the people "devoted themselves."

During this early stage of our crossing-over journey, I read my Bible with new eyes, and so will you. I wanted to reread even the most familiar passages of Scripture to look for anything I had missed. And there it was. In Acts 2:42 (NIV), I read the very first three words written about the newly emerging church community: *They devoted themselves.* I had always read past these three words, eager to see what they were devoted *to* without realizing where all this devotion was coming *from.* "They" were the people; the three thousand converts from the day of Pentecost. "They" were newly saved believers who devoted themselves to the apostles' teaching, to each other, and to their world.

These three words, "they devoted themselves," have been overlooked or undiscovered in many, if not all, of the studies that have been done about the early church's growth and influence. In all our research into how and why the early church exploded from Pentecost onwards, we have not studied the "who" factor. We've examined principles, patterns, leadership styles, and structures, but maybe we've missed the most important thing of all—the caliber of the people who *were* the early church.

We've examined principles, patterns, leadership styles, and structures, but maybe we've missed the most important thing of all—the caliber of the people who were the early church.

I suddenly realized that Acts 2:42–47 was not describing a church model or structure that could be copied; it was describing a *culture.* Throughout church history, God has been the same; His purpose and Word are the same in every generation. But we the church have not been the same;

the people in the church have been the only variable.

Every past move of God has only been as good as the people who partnered with God in it. The caliber, quality, and character of the church at any given time have been the unknown "X-factors." When God had quality people to work with, His purpose advanced in the earth; when He didn't, everything went on hold until the next usable generation of the church emerged. Genesis 6:8 tells us *God found Noah* (NIV), suggesting that God had been looking for someone to partner with, and He always is. It seems that sometimes throughout church history, God has lacked quality, committed people. We see this pattern everywhere in our spiritual history. A survey of Old Testament Israel's history reveals a roller-coaster story of good kings followed by bad kings, and as went the king, so went the fortunes of the nation.

In Acts 2:42 I had found the biblical beginnings of the kind of church I wanted to build; a *self-devoted* and responsibility-taking church. The church I had, and didn't want any-

78

more, was one in which the devotion, inspi-
ration, and motivation came from leadership
down to the people. But here in Acts, at the
headwaters of where we all came from, at the
roots of the New Testament church, was
something lost for centuries.

In the early church, the devotion, passion,
motivation, and commitment for life came
from the people. Somehow, two thousand
years later, that devotion has been transferred
from the people to leaders. Now we in leadership spend large amounts of time trying to
motivate, energize, and
encourage our people to
own the vision, serve,
attend, give, support, commit, and so on. Perhaps one
of our greatest problems in
the twenty-first century
church is what we as leaders spend our time doing. If
a New Testament church
leader dropped into today's western church,
he would be shocked at what most pastors
spend their time doing.

Perhaps one of our greatest problems in the twenty-first century church is what we as leaders spend our time doing.

Having decided that I would not allow the
church to rely on me to keep them devoted, I
began a dual process of "teaching the old
dogs new tricks" and preventing the "new
dogs" from learning old tricks. Many of the

people in our church lacked a personal root into God; instead, they had a "drinking straw" into each other! Networks of co-dependent relationships formed the culture of the church. Historically, our church leaders governed by emphasizing a covenant community church culture. I believe in covenant, but covenant without an outward focus can be lethal. And so began my redesign of our *cultural architecture,* fashioning the new church we were to become.

One of the first things I did to wean people off their leadership dependency was to instruct all our cell-group leaders to stop chasing people who didn't show up to their cell-group meetings. This was what we had done for years: phoning all non-attendees just to let them know we missed them and to remind them to be there next week. We were inadvertently creating a culture where people were taught to expect leaders to chase after them or be devoted for them.

Follow-Up

"Follow-up," as we tend to understand and practice it in the modern church, is not a biblical idea. I discovered that our follow-up team was spending all their time chasing after reluctant people who had raised a hand in a service, indicating a commitment to Christ, but then didn't come back. It was our culture to follow up with these people, but we were trying harder than they were to follow through on their decision. Our team would contact them, inform them of follow-up classes, offer transportation, counseling, home visitation, prayer, and so forth. We were more devoted to them making it than they were themselves! Again, we were modeling to these people that this was how things worked—you lift a hand, and we all run after you.

I searched the Scriptures for "follow-up" and couldn't find it. In fact, in the Bible people followed after Jesus, not the other way around. I expected to find "follow-up" in Acts 2 because three thousand new converts in one day would surely merit an elaborate follow-up system. But what I found was that "they devoted themselves"; I didn't find leaders going house-to-house in Jerusalem trying to get people plugged into the church. I looked for the follow-up of the poor guy

> *In the Bible people followed after Jesus, not the other way around.*

possessed by a legion of demons, whom we read about in Luke 8:26–39. Surely, if anyone needed some follow-up, a discipleship program, or a Foundation of Faith class, it would be this man. Instead, what we actually find is the man begging to go with Jesus, not Jesus begging him to follow Him (Luke 8:38). Rather than Jesus encouraging him to stick around Him and His team, Jesus tells him to go home and tell his story to everyone.

Please understand that I fully appreciate our responsibility to provide for those we reach with the gospel. I know the value of the basic courtesies of informing people about all we provide for them in the shape of follow-up resources. What I don't understand is why we try so hard to plug people into the church in a way which starts them on their Christian life with a wrong perception of how things work. Providing information is helpful; chasing down converts is not. If they begin to expect the attention, six months later, when we relax our follow-up toward them because by now we think they should be plugged in, they ask, "What happened to all the love in the church?" What they are really asking is, "What happened to all the attention I received because I've become dependent on it to keep me coming to church?" Our follow-up was motivated by a fear that if we didn't chase them, they wouldn't be back, rather than a faith that if they were genuinely born again, we wouldn't be able to keep them away.

Our follow-up was motivated by a fear that if we didn't chase them, they wouldn't be back, rather than a faith that if they were genuinely born again, we wouldn't be able to keep them away.

I gave my life to Christ at the age of fifteen. I was living at home with my parents, three brothers, and two sisters. My family was very antichurch, so I found those early months very difficult. But here's the point: I never received any follow-up. I had no telephone number to call, no transportation, no Bible, no money, and no Christian friends—yet I was in church twice a week. (In fact, I am still waiting for that "follow up!") Look what no follow-up did to me! I never *expected* any follow-up, and its absence never gave me a chance to become dependent on it. Again, my point is simply that two thousand years from the beginnings of the early church, the responsibility to follow Christ and be in the church community seems to have shifted from followers to leaders. We have made a burden for our own back.

All this was the prize that I fought for in crossing over—a church that was God-centered; a church that was devoted to Christ, each other, and the world; a church with a responsibility-taking, ownership culture—a "new breed church." People from across the world have said to me, "You could never build a church like that; people expect more from us than that—people wouldn't come if we didn't stay on their case." Well, to them I simply say, "Come and see the church you thought couldn't be built!"

Chapter 7

God's Carriers

Crossing over must first be conceptual before it can be practical. We must cross over our minds into new thoughts. Our minds need a conceptual, intellectual, "promised land." We believe with our hearts, but we behave with our heads, so for any new behavior to become established, our minds need to be fully convinced.

Crossing over demands rethinking the meaning of familiar words and concepts like membership, covenant, belonging, commitment, team, fellowship, and above all, leadership.

Leadership has predominantly become a badge, a label, and a title. In our historic church structure, we had a very clear leadership system extending from the Ephesians 4 ministries, local church elders, deacons, department heads, cell-group leaders, and so on. In fact, leadership was something we were renowned for and taught many others about. Our leadership wasn't wrong or bad or lacking—we had lots of leaders. It was just that despite having so many leaders, I felt completely alone in my leadership and couldn't understand why. How could I be alone when I was surrounded by leaders, had regular leaders' meetings, and employed staff to help me lead? It was this burning question that led me to examine Moses' life, and there I found my answer.

> *I felt completely alone in my leadership and couldn't understand why.*

Carriers

Despite Moses having hundreds of teachers, elders, tribal heads, and even his own brother and sister "on staff" with him, it would appear that he felt totally alone. His sense of loneliness, however, had nothing to do with numbers, resources, friends, or staffing; it was much deeper, and so was mine. I had leaders coming out of my ears with titles galore at the local, regional, national, and international levels. So why did I feel alone? Then I found it—I found my word, my concept, my new idea of leadership which both explained my aloneness and forever changed how I would look at leadership in the future. This word was used by Moses to explain his own sense of being alone. This word explained what was missing both in his church and mine. The word is "carry," and Moses used it to describe to God what he felt was missing in his world. In Numbers 11:10–15 (NIV) we read:

> *Moses heard the people of every family wailing, each at the entrance to his tent. The* Lord *became exceedingly angry, and Moses was troubled. He asked the* Lord, *"Why have you brought this trouble on your servant? What have I done to displease you that you put the burden of all these people on me? Did I conceive all these people? Did I give them birth? Why do you tell me to carry them in my arms,*

as a nurse carries an infant, to the land you promised on oath to their fore-fathers? Where can I get meat for all these people? They keep wailing to me, 'Give us meat to eat!' I cannot carry all these people by myself; the burden is too heavy for me. If this is how you are going to treat me, put me to death right now—if I have found favor in your eyes—and do not let me face my own ruin."

In one, hard-to-express, hard-to-explain, but fundamental area of his leadership, Moses felt alone. He felt alone in carrying the burden of the people. He didn't feel alone in leadership, company, or relationships, but in *carrying*. He summed up his feelings, "I cannot carry all these people by myself, it's too heavy for me."

Not all leaders are carriers, and not all carriers are the recognized leaders; that was my problem. I had many leaders, but most of them were not carrying anything. Although we were all handling the same burden, I felt as if no one else was lifting it. It's like taking a piano up a flight of stairs—everyone looks like they're carrying it but usually, only a few are actually taking the strain. Not all who touch the burden are carrying the burden, but all look like they are. Badges and titles give the appearance of carrying because they often describe what that person is responsible for, but carrying isn't about the badge—it's about bearing the burden. Moses had lots of leaders but no carriers.

Carrying Affects Your Walk

During this time of redefining leadership, I visited Africa and noticed just how many people carried their burdens. I watched an old lady on her way home through the town center. She must have been in her seventies, but she was carrying a huge bundle of fire-wood on her back. A strap attached to the wood stretched across her forehead, causing the weight of the load to bend her forward, straining her neck. The steeper the hill, the lower she bent until she could only see her feet. The next day I saw two young boys, probably around eight years old, trying to carry two sacks of maize home. In the sweltering heat they would drag the sacks a few feet, then stop and rest. It was around 10 a.m. when I passed them on the road to the town where I was speaking at that day. They were still dragging those sacks when I drove back around 5 p.m.

My understanding of carrying deepened with these observations: carrying affects your walk. Carrying affects your journey, your appearance, and your style. Carrying governs your time and slows you down. Carrying is hard work; it's the hardest part of the journey. That's exactly the reason why many people don't want to be carriers; they know that it will change their walk. I had discovered my new definition of leadership: *true leaders are carriers;* leaders don't walk like others; leaders travel with a burden, and leaders can only walk as fast as their burdens will allow.

True leaders are carriers.

I returned home from Africa looking differently at every leader and asking myself and them, "What are you carrying?" Each would answer me according to his or her job description, saying things like, "I'm carrying in the youth department," or kids' church, or worship team. This was the right answer, but it still left me feeling like no one was really carrying in those areas because I was constantly getting involved in those departments and sorting out problems. I was called on to recruit more people for them, to pray for resources, and to be constantly thinking about how to improve those areas. In fact, in some of the most overpopulated leadership areas of church life, I felt totally alone. Although there were many of us gathered around the "piano" of those ministry areas, it seemed I was the only one taking any of the weight.

The Stain on the Carpet

It was our monthly leadership night and all our staff, elders, group leaders, and department heads were gathering. As I entered the room and walked down the aisle to the front, I noticed a huge stain on the carpet. Seeing our caretaker, I asked him what it was. He replied that he hadn't noticed it before but thought it looked like cola, probably spilled during a youth service. It looked weeks old, was right in the middle of the aisle, and drove me nuts. All night, as I taught on what it meant to be a carrier, I couldn't get this stain off my mind. It really bothered me that a guy paid to fix it didn't even see it. And I wondered how many others hadn't seen it.

Eventually I asked my gathered leaders, "How many of you noticed that huge stain on the carpet when you walked in tonight?" In a room of about sixty people, seven hands went up. So fifty-three leaders hadn't even noticed it, and I felt angry about it but didn't understand why. "It is only a carpet stain, calm down, chill out," my reasonable side kept telling me. So I asked, "How many of you seven who saw it did anything about it?" No hands went up, and I was getting angrier but clearer about why this stain mattered so much to me that I would allow it to consume so much of our monthly leaders' meeting. Then I asked—and by this time I was getting positively obsessive about it—"How many of you would notice a stain like that on your carpet at home?" Almost every hand went up, and those that didn't were probably telling the truth because I had been in their homes. Then, my final question: "If you would notice and clean it in your house, why wouldn't you clean it in God's house?" The answer to that question was the final focusing adjustment on the lens I was looking through. People effectively said: "It's not my responsibility."

That mind-set forms the basis of the difference between a carrier and a non-carrier. Carriers feel responsible for everything, whether it's their responsibility by title, badge, or position. They obsess over things nobody has asked them to. Carriers see everything, feel everything, and want to be sure everything's been covered. The next day I, the senior pastor, got down on my hands and knees and cleaned the stain, and it became the most important stain in my life. That stain was a parable in helping me to find some of the new conceptual language for our crossing over. People seeing me cleaning would come over and insist that I let them do it, to which I ungraciously replied, "Why haven't you done it before?"

Carriers notice the stain and either take care of it themselves or see to it that it gets done. Carriers see the piece of litter in the car lot and pick it up; they don't ignore it because it's not their litter or their responsibility to pick it up. Carriers don't say, "We probably employ someone to do that"; they do it when they see it. Carriers notice dead flowers nobody has changed and flaky paint no one has fixed; fingerprints on the glass and dust on the woodwork; the light bulb that's out and the workman sawing wood without sweeping up! They notice waste, excess, carelessness, and sloppiness, which drives them crazy. They notice all these things effortlessly as they pass through a building, even though their minds are sup-

Carriers see the bigger picture instantly and notice the litter on the floor, and to them both are inextricably linked.

posed to be on bigger things. Carriers see the bigger picture instantly *and* notice the litter on the floor, and to them both are inextricably linked. Carriers are awesome and awful, both at the same time.

The Immature Only Carry What They Need

When my wife and I picked our children up from school, it was amazing how within moments of seeing them, they would start handing over everything they didn't want to carry. Parents were packhorses to carry their books, bags, coats, and shoes; all got transferred to Mom and Dad so the child could be free to play. It's a mark of immaturity to carry only what you must, whereas the mature carry many things that aren't their responsibility. Everything you carry beyond what you need for yourself is a mark of your carrier heart.

World War III could be unleashed in our home over the simple question, "Whose cup is that?" The children would rather argue over whose cup it was than just move it. Maturity just picks up the cup in passing, without giving a thought to who last drank from it and left it there. Churches across the world are overstaffed with people employed to "pick up cups" that wouldn't need picking up if their present staff and leadership were carriers. The "cup" is everyone's responsibility, and non-carriers hate that thought because it may involve them doing things they feel others should be doing.

Our problem is that there are always more cups in the cupboard than there are people who live in the house—hospitality dictates that. The apostle Paul, when writing to Timothy, points out that in a large house—and God's house is the largest of all—there are all kinds of useful vessels—some gold, some silver, some wood, and some clay (2 Timothy 2:20). What's important to God, Paul said, was not the appearance of the vessel but its usefulness. God doesn't have special china or porcelain in His house, only vessels for use. However, the church is full of "special china" Christians who make an appearance on special occasions, then return to the display case to continue being admired.

As a child, I remember one hot summer's day waiting for my older brother to finish with a cup so I could use it to drink from— we were always short of cups. I remember staring at the special china behind the glass door of the display cabinet thinking how ridiculous it was that what we needed was in the house but untouchable, due to its special status. My mother's mentality was "it's for special occasions," but I never remember any occasion being special enough because we never used it! Her logic went something like this: it's special, and special things stop being special if you use them too much. Well, to all the "special china" in the church cupboard I say, "You're not special, and we need your help; you're a vessel for use, not an ornament to be admired. You were created by the potter to carry things, and we have a big world to reach."

God's Answer to Moses

We started this chapter by reading Moses' lengthy appeal to God about his loneliness in his leadership task. Now let's turn to God's answer in Numbers 11:16–17:

> The LORD said to Moses: "Bring me
> seventy of Israel's elders who are
> known to you as leaders and officials
> among the people. Have them come
> to the Tent of Meeting, that they may
> stand there with you. I will come
> down and speak with you there, and
> I will take of the Spirit that is on you
> and put the Spirit on them. They will
> help you carry the burden of the peo-
> ple so that you will not have to carry
> it alone.

God promised him that they would help carry the burden of the people so that Moses would not have to carry it alone. Awesome! But how would that happen? It would happen only when they felt for the church as Moses did. And how could that happen? That could only happen if God took what was on Moses and put it on others. That's exactly what God did, and suddenly their eyes were opened to all the "stains on the carpet" they had been missing for years!

May a "carrier spirit" be on you and your church.

May a "carrier spirit" be on you and your church. May God take what's on your senior leadership, your Moses, and put it on you. If you are a Moses reading this, then hold on; help is at hand. God will somehow put your heart into them and your eyes over theirs, so they will feel, see, and do just as you do.

Chapter 8

All-Inclusive Living

The crossing-over process began by clarifying the kind of church we did and didn't want. Then we began implementing the conceptual shifts required to turn "The Church I See" into reality. This was what I referred to in chapter 6 as my *cultural architecture* of the new church we were becoming; it is all about developing culture, not creating new structures. This new culture embodied a "they devoted themselves" worldview and began producing a community of "carriers." But the culture was not yet fully formed. In particular, our attitudes toward the spiritually lost and socially disenfranchised had to be worked on. This is the focus of the next two chapters.

Prior to crossing over, our church was relatively exclusive; we were certainly not all-inclusive. The church consisted mainly of white, middle-income, middle-class people. We were religious, inward-looking, and definitely seeker-*in*sensitive. If I wasn't convinced of this prior to crossing over, I certainly was after we started our bus ministry. When we began bussing in people from the poorer parts of town, all hell broke loose in the church!

Our churches cannot be any bigger than our circle of love or our circle of inclusion. This truth became clear to me when God spoke to me through an unusual happening at our home. We were hosting a party in our old seventeenth-century farmhouse in the countryside. We don't have enough parking space for everyone on our land, so we park our guests on spare ground across the narrow country lane opposite our home. It was dark and cold. One member of our team named Robbie was out on the lane waving guests into the parking area using a flashlight to direct the traffic. When all the

Our churches cannot be any bigger than our circle of love or our circle of inclusion.

guests had gathered at the house and Robbie had come in from the cold, I asked him if everything went smoothly parking all the cars. He replied that everything was fine, except for one lady driving up the lane whom he had mistakenly waved into the party parking area! Assuming she was a party guest, Robbie saw her headlights and simply waved her in. Only when he approached the car to open the door did the distressed lady shout from her window, "Who are you, and why have you brought me here?" Realizing his mistake, Robbie apologized and waved her back out.

The moment he told me that story God said to me, "I want you to build that same mentality into your church."

I replied, "Lord, what mentality?"

"The mentality that assumes everyone is coming to the party."

Then I realized the incredible power of living an all-inclusive life, a life that accepts all people and simply includes them as if they are coming to the party. You see, we hadn't given Robbie a list of whom we were expecting with everyone's car number plate, so he just assumed that anyone driving up that country lane was a guest. Churches have been asking God for a list of whom He's expecting for decades;

It's more important to know whom God's loving than whom God's specifically inviting.

we often do this by asking God for a word of knowledge about some stranger or for a divine appointment. While I believe in both these things, I also believe that it's more important to know whom God's loving than whom God's specifically inviting.

Waving Them In

Robbie's assumption that night on the country lane demonstrated another simple but powerful reality: He removed the issue of choice from the lady he waved in. His all-inclusive mind-set only involved waving people in; it didn't involve first asking them whether they wanted to come in.

Jesus told the story of a great banquet where the party began by invitation but ended up being a party for everyone:

Jesus replied: "A certain man was preparing a great banquet and invited

*many guests. At the time of the ban-
quet he sent his servant to tell those
who had been invited, "Come, for
everything is now ready." But they all
alike began to make excuses.*

*The first said, "I have just bought a
field, and I must go and see it. Please
excuse me." Another said, "I have just
bought five yoke of oxen, and I'm on
my way to try them out. Please
excuse me." Still another said, "I just
got married, so I can't come."*

*The servant came back and
reported this to his master. Then the
owner of the house became angry
and ordered his servant, "Go out
quickly into the streets and alleys of
the town and bring in the poor, the
crippled, the blind and the lame."*

*"Sir," the servant said, "what you
ordered has been done, but there is
still room."*

*Then the master told his servant, "Go
out to the roads and country lanes and
make them come in, so that my house
will be full. I tell you, not one of those
men who were invited will get a taste of
my banquet"* (Luke 14:16–24 NIV).

Notice how all the invited people made
their excuses and cancelled, but that didn't
cause the host, who is a picture of God, to
cancel the party. Instead, he moved from people he knew to people he didn't and who

never dreamt that they would be invited to such a banquet, giving his servants the command to throw their circle of love and inclusion even wider by going out into the country lanes, just like the one where I live, and "make them come in." What a strange phrase; how can someone be *made* to come in? It sounds manipulative and cultish, until you remember how Robbie made that lady come into his world.

We make people do things all the time without even realizing it by simply removing the choice element. The other day I got into an elevator and had to stop for people at three floors on the way to mine. Every time I've eaten from a buffet, I have paid for everything I don't like as well as the food I do like. Buffets are all-inclusive menus, and the management doesn't give a discount for the dishes you don't like. The church of Jesus Christ is more like a buffet than a set meal, but some stand by that buffet complaining to God about all the people types they don't like, as if God will offer them an à la carte menu instead. Life is full of examples of people making us do what, if asked, we wouldn't do.

So instead of asking the poor of our city, "Do you want us to help you?" we just help them, feed them, clothe them, and include them—and none have yet said, "Stop!" Instead of asking our church if they want us to bring in the poor, homeless, alcoholics, addicts, or prostitutes, we just do it, and they sit next to each other in the services. They don't get to choose.

Circles of Love

When we live with all-inclusive hearts, we will bless far more people by accident than we ever would have on purpose. Jesus fed five thousand people including many who were against Him, didn't like Him, and would one day shout "crucify Him." When Paul and Silas's chains fell off, so did everyone else's. When God rescued Paul from his shipwreck, He rescued everyone on board with him. These and many others were all-inclusive miracles, miracles people didn't get to choose to be part of. God just included them because that's what God is like; He includes people.

> *When we live with all-inclusive hearts, we will bless far more people by accident than we ever would have on purpose.*

In Mark 9:39–41 we read of a situation in which the disciples stopped a man casting out a demon for no other reason than he wasn't in their group. Jesus rebuked them effectively saying *Do not forbid him, for no one who works a miracle in My name can soon afterward speak evil of Me. For he who is not against us is on our side. For whoever gives you a cup of water to drink in My name, because you belong to Christ, assuredly, I say to you, he will by no means lose his reward.* The disciples' circle of love was "just us," whereas Jesus' circle of love was "anyone who isn't against us." Wow! Those are two very different sized circles. Jesus' circle extends to even recognizing a small gesture like a cup of water; the disciple's circle couldn't see beyond their group. The awful implications of the disciples' exclusiveness was that it was better for the demon to stay in the person rather than for someone "not of our group" to cast it out. I wonder how many people remain unreached in our communities because of the same territorial small-mindedness in churches.

Jesus told us in His parable of the net, in Matthew 13:47, that when God goes fishing, He doesn't use a pole but a net. Fishing poles are exclusive, nets are inclusive. A net isn't choosy and isn't careful; a net doesn't try to control what it catches; it first includes, then the fishermen sort the contents. If God had just used a pole, maybe you would never have been caught because maybe nobody was fishing for your type. Nobody was fishing for the poor and hurting in Jesus' day, only Him, and thousands swam into His kingdom net.

> Nobody was fishing for the poor and hurting in Jesus' day, only Him, and thousands swam into His kingdom net.

Finally, I think it's important to understand that none of us are immune from needing to hear this. The great apostle Peter clearly struggled with a limited circle of love that didn't extend to the Gentiles. On the day of Pentecost, Peter preached a sermon that was all-inclusive, but he had real problems overcoming the expectations borne of his Jewish heritage. Peter, like many churches including ours before we crossed over, had a theology of inclusiveness but lived an exclusive lifestyle. It got so bad that Paul had to confront Peter in public in Antioch about his hypocrisy with the Gentiles (see Galatians 2:11).

It was only years later at the home of Cornelius, a Gentile centurion, that Peter finally realized just how big God's circle of love was. In his vision a few days earlier, where he saw a sheet let down from heaven three times with all kinds of unclean animals in it that he was commanded to "kill and eat," Peter's refusal to love and accept everyone had been totally condemned by God. A voice spoke from heaven saying, "Don't call anything unclean or impure that God has made clean." This was all a set-up to prepare him for his visit to the home of the Gentile Cornelius. The Acts of the Apostles records how Peter told those gathered at Cornelius' house, *In truth I perceive that God shows no partiality. But in every nation whoever fears Him and works righteousness is accepted by Him* (Acts 10:34–35).

Peter spent three years with Jesus. Years later he realized how big God's love really was. On the Mount of Transfiguration, Peter said, *You are the Christ, the son of the living God* (Matthew 16:16)—a revelation that Jesus confirmed. "Revelation" and "realization" are two different things. Revelation is God showing you something you didn't know. Realization is you understanding something you already knew but didn't know you knew until circumstances helped you discover it.

Eight years ago I realized that our church's circle of love was too small, and that realization changed our church and me forever. Millions stay away from our churches because they think they would never be accepted. But we don't include people because they're acceptable *to us*; we include them because they are already accepted *by God.* None of us are acceptable, but all of us are accepted by God. The issue of acceptance is not ours to decide. God says, "Whosoever will" may come and drink of the water of life (see Revelation 22:17). The bigger your circle, the more people can come to God. God so loved the world—all of it—that He sent Jesus, and now Jesus has sent you and me.

Chapter 9

The Family of the Unsandaled

As we have continued on our crossing over journey, the conviction that we must be an all-inclusive church has only deepened. More than ever we are determined not to be "The Family of the Unsandaled." This was a name that spoke of shame, selfishness, and disgrace in Deuteronomy 25. Although God would not want this said of anyone, it was God Himself who gave this name to certain family lines and here's why:

If brothers are living together and one of them dies without a son, his widow must not marry outside the family. Her husband's brother shall take her and marry her and fulfill the duty of a brother-in-law to her. The first son she bears shall carry on the name of the dead brother so that his name will not be blotted out from Israel. However, if a man does not want to marry his brother's wife, she shall go to the elders at the town gate and say, "My husband's brother refuses to carry on his brother's name in Israel. He will not fulfill the duty of a brother-in-law to me."

Then the elders of his town shall summon him and talk to him. If he persists in saying, "I do not want to marry her," his brother's widow shall go up to him in the presence of the elders, take off one of his sandals, spit in his face and say, "This is what is done to the man who will not build up his brother's family line."

That man's line shall be known in Israel as The Family of the Unsandaled" (Deuteronomy 25:5–10 NIV).

Here we see that from the beginning, it was God's intention for the processes of restoration and recovery to be built into the community of His people. At the heart of this brother-in-law's duty to marry his brother's widow was not charity, welfare, or pity but the opportunity for restoration and recovery

from what would other-
wise become a life-domi-
nating problem.

From the beginning, it was God's intention for restoration and recovery to be built into the community of His people.

To be widowed without
children was to have your
family line cut short and
your husband's name erased
from history. *The first son
she bears shall carry on
the name of the dead brother, so that his
name will not be blotted out from Israel*
(Deuteronomy 25:6 NIV).

God made helping this widow an issue of
duty and obligation; He didn't leave it to
chance, choice, or convenience. God built
this principle of recovery for widows into the
spiritual and moral DNA of His people. This
distinguished them from widows in other
societies who lacked the benefit of this value,
who would never recover from their families'
losses. This duty to restore the broken among
His people was the envy of every other
nation. If life dealt you the crushing blow of
bereavement without progeny, then those
closest to you would make it their responsibility to step in and guarantee your recovery,
removing the fear that widowhood could
become a life-dominating condition.

God's heart for people meant that the possibility of recovery was in place before the

God's heart for people meant that the possibility of recovery was in place before the need for it ever arose.

need for it ever arose. So in the years following this young woman's bereavement, no one would ever know of her huge loss because her restoration within the community had protected both her identity and that of her future children, who would never be perceived as being different from any others.

God Thinks and Acts Generationally

When God instituted this principle of recovery, His primary concern was for the preservation and future prosperity of the dead man's family line.

God established that the consequences for the brother-in-law who refused to help would be so serious, they would carry generational consequences. This brother-in-law was not just refusing to help his brother's widow, but he was refusing to preserve and continue his brother's name and lineage. His sin was not just against the living widow and his dead brother, but also against those who would never be born without his intervention. Dealing with the drama and public disgrace associated with his refusal to help was one thing, but the generational stigma of being known as The Family of the Unsandaled, the family that refused to help, was meant to be unbearable. To be so named was to be identified as a family who cared neither for those hurting today nor for those who would suffer tomorrow.

To be willing to be publicly named, shamed, spat on, and unsandaled was in effect admitting that you had no real understanding of God's covenant community or God's heart for His people. It made you a misfit. This deterrent was huge—as huge as God's heart for the hurting and the broken.

The Church of the Unsandaled

Overcoming the disasters and setbacks we sometimes face in life is not always our personal and exclusive responsibility. God has placed us in a covenant community—the church—and without the help of the church around us, we too might never recover.

Our church family contains hundreds of stories of recovery. Whether recovering from divorce, bereavement, addictions, bankruptcy, or abuse, these people have somehow found a way back to living a full and happy life with the help of a church who has refused to be known as the Church of the Unsandaled. Our leadership has committed to build restoration and recovery into the DNA of our house, and that is why so many lives have recovered from things that became no more than temporary setbacks, when the potential was there to destroy them completely.

Our joy is that many of those we have helped restore, by fulfilling the duty of the brother-in-law, have now gone on to live extraordinarily generous lives. From their once-broken lives have come ideas, initiatives, and ministries that are now reaching thousands. These to whom we refused to become The Family of the Unsandaled have themselves refused to become the unsandaled to others.

God could name thousands of churches across the world "The Family of the Unsandaled." As long as the church continues to shoot its own wounded, rather than help them to recover, we can't begin to help the plight of the millions outside the church who will not recover without our help. To a hurting world much of the church is no better than the brother-in-law in whose face the widow spat. In fact, the world has every right to, as it were, spit in the face of any church which, despite seeing its community ravaged by sin, does nothing. May it never be said of our church or yours that we have become The Family of the Unsandaled to our community.

> *May it never be said of our church or yours that we have become The Family of the Unsandaled to our community.*

Tsunami Orphans

Tens of thousands of families lost loved ones in the Southeast Asian tsunami on December 26, 2004. Thousands of children were orphaned overnight and faced life without parents, a life worse than death in some cultures of the world.

I was very moved while watching TV footage in the hours and days following the disaster. What moved me most was how many of the surviving parents collected orphaned children from their village. It didn't matter to them that the children weren't their own children; what mattered was that these kids would not face life without a mom and dad. The tsunami was devastating, but it would not be allowed to dominate the life of the next generation. These non-believers shamed much of the church by what they did; they refused, as did the Good Samaritan, to walk by those who were hurting and instead chose to get involved in their world. Despite the agony of their own loss of loved ones, they reached out and began to love others back to recovery.

Like many churches, we sent money to the tsunami appeal, as we did to the victims of Hurricane Katrina, the Rwandan genocide, and the Pakistani earthquake. However, none of that must ever become a substitute for completing our responsibility to the hurting, poor, and oppressed on our own doorstep. It's much easier to send aid across the world than to become aid where we live. The "tsunami of sin" and all its consequences are destroying our communities, one life at a time. The bereaved, empty, and desperate single parent, who will cry herself to sleep again tonight, needs to know about you, your

It's much easier to send aid across the world than to become aid where we live.

church, and the family of God. What the
devil meant for evil, God can turn to good
through the love of a "search and rescue"
church, one committed to the restoration and
recovery of all within its immediate sphere of
influence. The duty of the brother-in-law has
now fallen to us.

It is often reported to us by people who
visit our church from out of town, that when
they stop to ask strangers for directions, not
only do people know who we are but they
often say, "That's the place that helps people." If that was the only thing our city ever
said about our church, I would consider it the
greatest compliment they could ever give us.
What do they say about your church?

The Kinsman-redeemer

The kinsman-redeemer was the closest living
male relative to a widowed family member.
We are introduced to the concept in Ruth
4:3–12. Anyone experiencing the loss of a
husband, and who perhaps had no brother-in-
law, could still be rescued by the intervention
of a kinsman-redeemer. Boaz became kinsman-redeemer to Ruth, a widowed Moabite

woman who had chosen to stay with her widowed mother-in-law, Naomi, when Naomi returned to Bethlehem after the death of her husband and sons.

What you make happen for others, God will make happen for you. So what Ruth did for Naomi, God made sure that Boaz did for Ruth. Never forget that God not only wants to bless the one being helped but also the one helping, whom God will bless with more than enough to provide for those He has chosen to "redeem." Economics was never a valid reason for refusing to help redeem another person, and it's still not a valid reason for any church to not help its community today. The decision to help the poor, the hurting, and the broken is the best economic decision any church can ever make.

> *The decision to help the poor, the hurting, and the broken is the best economic decision any church can ever make.*

May You Be Blessed Like Perez

After his redeeming of Ruth, the elders of Bethlehem proclaimed this blessing over

Boaz: *May your house be like the house of Perez, whom Tamar bore to Judah, because of the offspring which the* LORD *will give you from this young woman* (Ruth 4:12).

Perez was one of the twin boys born to Tamar—whose story we learned in chapter 4. Tamar had children through Judah, her father-in-law and reluctant kinsman-redeemer, and one of them she named Perez, which means "I have broken out." Perez became the father of a family dynasty that reached straight into Christ's own genealogy (Matthew 1:3).

Ruth, a widowed outsider, and Perez, the son of a woman whom no one would help, both ended up in Christ's genealogy. Those who had no family line found one through others who stepped in to help them recover. Such is the heart of God! He refused to become The Family of the Unsandaled to either Tamar or Ruth and included them in His own family line.

Without our help, multiplied millions of lost people will never make it into Christ's family line of faith. With our help, as their spiritual brothers-in-law or as kinsman-redeemers, they can recover not only from the blows life has dealt them but also go on to become the restorers of others. To every believer, pastor, and church who will take

121

this message to heart, I want to say on behalf of every Tamar, Perez, Ruth, and Naomi living in your community, "Thank you for refusing to be The Family of the Unsandaled. Thank you for building a life and a church of restoration, recovery, and second chances." This spirit is at the core of a crossed over church.

Chapter 10

God's Dot-to-Dot
Connections

Sadly, the first casualty of any crossing over
will be relationships. People who don't feel
they can embrace change
or buy into the new order
will leave those who do,
and vice versa. This is
scary to those of us who
place a high value on relationships and have spent
years of our lives investing
in and working on our
relationships. The realiza-

*The realization that
not all who now
travel with us on our
faith journey will do
so in the future is
more than some can
bear.*

tion that not all who now travel with us on our faith journey will do so in the future is more than some can bear. The will of God divides as well as unites people, not intentionally, but as a consequence of its various demands on our lives.

In this chapter I want to say something about my own background and the centrality of certain relationships from which I had to walk away. I'm talking about this because the overwhelming fear of going forward without some people, and especially those whom you once looked up to, can be paralyzing.

I was born again in 1972 at the age of fifteen through the witness of a schoolteacher. I came from a completely unchurched background, which is true of most people in the UK today. That schoolteacher became my first mentor, and within a year or so of leading me to Christ, he entered full-time ministry in what was the beginning of the old church we have since crossed over. He and his older brother, together with others, pioneered what became known as the House Church movement in our country. It was a few years into the Charismatic Renewal which began in the late 1960s, and people from all denominations were being baptized in the Spirit, speaking in tongues, and leaving their established churches. These people regrouped in homes where they met for worship, fellowship, and prayer, and without any denominational restraints, began to flourish. It was real New Testament stuff; we met together from house to house, broke bread, and heard the Word of God taught by non-ordained but anointed people.

As Jonathan, King Saul's son, had tasted the honey in the woods and felt renewed (1 Samuel 14:27–29), our eyes had brightened. There was no going back. We were redefining church in our country and thousands upon thousands were leaving the mainline denominations to be a part of this new movement.

Covenant Relationships

The glue between all of us was no longer based on denominational loyalties or church structures; it was simply relational. We were outlawed effectively by the religious status quo and that deepened the bond between us. Our leaders were called apostles (then, a new term in the modern church), and their courage, wisdom, and commitment were breathtaking. These apostles were committed to the restoration of the true nature of the church, which was summed up in often-used phrases like "being a covenant community of God's people." We didn't go to church, we were the church; we didn't attend a service and go home, we were a spiritual family who lived life together. Ordained leaders didn't care for us, we cared for each other; our loyalty wasn't to a denomination but to the community of God's people. We were in covenant together, made ourselves accountable to each other, and spoke into each other's lives at a deep level. Our leadership style was later referred to as "heavy shepherding," which it probably was, although that wasn't how we saw it at the time. Our closeness and intimacy was perhaps the envy of all who simply attended church but felt lonely in life. We cherished our closeness and many, many lives were rescued and made better because of it.

From the beginning, my life was marked by the apostles as having leadership potential. From my twenties onward, I was privileged to be mentored, discipled, and fathered by those apostles. The senior apostle and I became so close that he became the father I never had and I became his spiritual son, in whom he saw his apostolic succession continuing. He was my hero, and I loved him deeply; he was a spiritual giant, and his company was the joy of my life. His greatest gift to me was his belief in me; it was so strong it made me and others believe in me. To hear him preach and watch him administer wisdom to leaders was truly awesome. He had the heart of a pioneer and the soul of a poet, and every time he preached those two rivers merged into what at times became mesmerizing eloquence—boy could he preach! I entered into full-time ministry with him in 1982, and we spent the next sixteen years building the church and advancing the kingdom of God together.

I'm trying to paint a picture for you of my relational background, and the primary impression I want to communicate is one of a deep, loving, covenant nature. All of this is so important for you to understand because of what happened during the early stages of my crossing over. My spiritual father didn't approve and wouldn't endorse my sense of calling to build differently than he did. The church I saw kept all the good things of our past but would not include the bad

The church I saw kept all the good things of our past but would not include the bad things that had developed in more recent years.

things that had developed in more recent years. Things like a controlling leadership style and failure to endorse and release the next generation of leaders to their destinies were breeding nationwide unrest within the network of churches. I think the apostles saw our emerging circle of influence *within* theirs, but I saw our circles more like the Olympic rings. There would be areas where our circles overlapped—shared projects, joint events, and much common ground. But there would also be parts of our circles that didn't overlap—our own distinct spheres of influence which differentiated between us. It was this degree of independence that was perceived as a threat to our long-established relationship and ultimately led to its frag-mentation.

Dot-to-Dot

By late 1998, my relationship with my spiri-tual father was all but over, yet I was on the brink of the greatest challenge of my life. How I needed his wisdom! We were for the first time in twenty-five years without any apostolic covering, a cardinal sin to anyone from our background. Throughout our country we were labeled "independent," "rebellious," "divisive," and "disloyal." I was a covenant breaker, the worst thing anybody could be accused of. I, and those who stuck with me, became spiritual lepers overnight; we were the rebels in the north, the church stealers. From the age of fifteen, these men of God had been my world, men I assumed I would grow old with. Now here I was orphaned overnight and feeling responsible for all who stayed with me.

Some of the leaders around me, no doubt feeling the increasing rejection of us, suggested we reach out to another apostle for covering and government. I could fully understand this suggestion; it would have at least made us appear accountable relationally and perhaps would have lessened the outcry against us. I just knew that this would have been a wrong move, yet I felt badly that I was offering no alternative.

One day as I was praying about all this, God reminded me of the dot-to-dot pictures that I did as a child. You know, the ones where you draw a line between each numbered dot and eventually an image appears. I remember as a kid thinking that the dots were placed wrong. The number two dot was too far away from the one dot, the six from the seven, etc. I guess I had already decided in my mind what the image was going to be, and for that reason I thought the dots were in the wrong places. Eventually, I connected the dots and the image came forth. Through this memory, God spoke to me. I felt God say so clearly, "Paul, I am going to include you in my global dot-to-dot relationship picture. If you don't fight Me over where the dots are placed, as you did when you were a kid, I will connect you to other people on the planet who are also part of My global dot-to-dot relational matrix." I shared this with my team, and as weak and simplistic as it seemed to be, it was enough to stabilize us for a few months and help us avoid making a relational miscalculation by joining some other apostolic network.

Seven years later, those dots have developed and are cross-continental, cross-denominational, and defy definition. These new relationships are, I think, a new relational wineskin. They are not governmental or structural, just relational and practical. Whomever you are looking for but cannot find is also looking for you, and God will connect your dots.

Far more is being achieved in the earth by practical relationship than by structural government. Far more is happening by friendships than authority. Far more is happening by brothering than fathering. Growing up in my natural family, I owed far more to brothering than fathering. Although we have lacked fathers in the church, what we often call fathering is simply the role of older brothers. My older brothers saved my life on numerous occasions when I was growing up by simply passing on to me (without authority or position) things their few years' experience had taught them. As I write this, I haven't had a spiritual father like the one I described earlier for almost ten years, but I have had some older brothering, which has been enough. If the fathers won't empower and release the sons, then the sons will have to leave home and find each other.

Far more is being achieved in the earth by practical relationship than by structural government. Far more is happening by friendships than authority.

If the fathers won't empower and release the sons, then the sons will have to leave home and find each other.

The first murder in human history was between brothers, Cain and Abel. That original assault on brotherhood speaks to me of a loss at the beginning of time that we must see restored. I am aware of so many pastors who, while they yearn for a spiritual leader, wouldn't dream of reaching out to an older brother in their own town. We line up for an appointment with the "fathers" but don't speak to our brothers in the line. My greatest release as a parent was the help my older children gave to the younger. That leadership within my own house didn't threaten, compete with, or undermine my leadership. My children would tell each other things they would never tell me, and some of those things became lifesaving conversations. We have celebrated fathering, but perhaps undervalued brothering. For some reading this who are like me and like Joshua, your fathers will not cross over with you, but you must go on.

My spiritual father died four years ago at the age of sixty-three. On the rare occasions I saw him prior to his death, he would always tell me how proud he was of me and how he watched me on TV. Though I really appreciated that, it was all too little too late; it was support long after I most needed it, and therein lies the story of all too many father-son relationships. I miss him. The church and the planet are worse off without him. But I must keep going and finish my race, and so must you.

Release the Youth

God told me at the outset of crossing over to empower and release the youth. So I did. Now, as I reach my mid-life, I am surrounded by the youth I empowered. They are my staff, my leaders, and above all, my friends. Some are preaching all over the world. Some are writing songs and albums now being sung around the world. Some are carrying a huge responsibility in ministry. In some places I am introduced by my connection to them, as if they discovered me, and I love it. My spiritual kids are living their dreams, they are getting to do some of the things I now do, but they're doing it at least ten years ahead of when I first did it.

I refuse to get in their way. I refuse to be responsible for dropping the baton. We are running together and will for years to come. But my legacy, my future, is already secure in them. They will go further, deeper, and wider than me; they will have a circle outside of mine, but part of it will overlap with mine. God, help me to help them live their dreams. May I never be a hindrance to their progress; may I grow old watching my children and theirs shaking the planet for You. Amen!

Chapter 11

Without a Complaint Your Vision Will Perish

The concepts and practical lessons I have shared in this book are fleshed out in the life of our church today. It is awesome. But then I am biased! Conceptual shifts have become concrete actions and shaped a "new breed" church. This vibrant, thriving community is increasingly becoming "The Church I See" and changing our city. The culture is established, and all who join us quickly become infected by it. Increasingly, our challenge is not to keep creating the culture but to sustain the momentum we have gathered. Many churches enjoy a "growth push" but then settle back into mediocrity.

How then do we sustain our momentum? By having within the strands of our spiritual DNA the two attitudes I want to explore as we bring this book to its conclusion. They are:

- A commitment to understand and keep in touch with the complaint that fuels your personal vision
- A commitment to live full and die empty

Write the vision and make it plain on tablets, that he may run who reads it (Habakkuk 2:2). This is probably one of the best-known and most quoted verses in the Bible on the subject of vision. However, what is usually less-known is the context within which it was spoken. These words from God to Habakkuk were part of a reply to some specific issues Habakkuk had been asking God about. Habakkuk 1 records these complaints which had become the focus of his anger and frustration. His complaints were about injustice, lawlessness, the oppression of the poor, and how the wicked seemed to be getting away with murder—often literally.

Habakkuk had table-thumping, finger-wagging, voice-raising complaints that he would not leave alone until he heard from God. He was in good company. His contemporary, Jeremiah, had a similar complaint, as did Nehemiah, Moses, and Gideon. More recent history records that Abraham Lincoln had a complaint about slavery, Martin Luther King, Jr. had a complaint about racism, Nelson Mandela had a complaint about apartheid, Mother Teresa had a complaint about hunger and poverty, and the list goes on. All were so motivated by their complaints that they gave their lives to doing something about them, and their work became their visions.

> *At the core of every visionary leader's life is a deep dissatisfaction with how things are. At the root of every history maker's calling is a complaint. That complaint is his or her cause, fuel, drive, and motivation.*

The principle I am therefore establishing is this: At the core of every visionary leader's life is a deep dissatisfaction with how things are. At the root of every history maker's calling is a complaint. That complaint is his or her cause, fuel, drive, and motivation to press through and accomplish the dream, however tough it gets along the way.

I want you to understand this important principle because in Christian teaching and preaching, our emphasis is usually on the vision, not the complaint it sprang from. We study vision, are keen to ask what a person's vision is, and work hard to "communicate the vision" of our church, ministry, or organization. However, unless that vision springs from a fundamental dissatisfaction with how things are, it lacks a cause. And without a cause, vision lacks a "why?" It lacks a reason.

The vision you have will perish and die unless you stay in vital touch with the complaint that first motivated you to develop a vision of a better future and then do something about it.

People need a reason to sacrifice for the vision you are presenting, and that reason must be real, known, and felt by all involved. They must feel the strength of the complaint which fuels the vision. And here lies the point of this chapter: The vision you have will perish and die unless you stay in vital touch with the complaint that first motivated you to develop a vision of a better future and then do something about it. Without a complaint, your vision will perish.

Complaint or Compliant

When people have no complaint, they become compliant; they do what others tell them, accept the status quo, and sign up to long-established traditions. They do what they do because everyone else does; together they comply.

Compliant people will never become visionary people. Compliant leaders cannot be visionary leaders because compliance is comfortable and comfort has never been the mother of complaint. A comfortable church without any complaints is doomed, even if it has a clear vision statement and a reputation as a visionary church. Many churches have a clear vision statement with no apparent influence on the day-to-day activities of the church. Much of the leader's time is spent talking about the vision to staff, the wider leadership, and the congregation, but with little success. Life becomes a continuous struggle to get more people involved with the vision. The vision is clear and well articulated, but people remain inactive. Why? The reason is simple: to share my vision, you must first share my complaint. Once you share my complaint, envisioning is easy.

Until you feel what I feel about what's wrong, you will never understand why you should help me put it right.

Vision is fueled from two directions, the past and the future. My complaint about what must change pushes from behind, and my vision of better things pulls me forward. The gift this gives me is awesome: on a bad day, or whenever I feel overwhelmed by the size of the challenge of the future, I will always keep going by simply remembering the past.

To share my vision, you must first share my complaint.

From late 1998 on, we began crossing our church over from the safe, comfortable, and controlling church we were, to the "new breed" church we've become. Today it sometimes feels as if our church membership has a "pre" and "post" crossing over mixture to it. Those who were in the church prior to 1998 can remember the past, and those who arrived in more recent years cannot. Some of us feel like war veterans sometimes, and the freedoms we fought and suffered for make us just as scared about going back as others are excited about going forward. If we ever have moments of doubt or lack confidence about going forward, we only have to remember the past—which we are determined never to go back to—and going forward suddenly becomes a great option, however great the challenge we face! People who haven't realized going back is never better will always struggle to find a reason to keep going in the face of adversity.

Back is never better. History is not kind to people who go back. The Bible does not record what happened to people who went back; it simply forgets them. God is not interested in the "Orpahs" who go back but in the "Ruths" who know that forward is the only option (Ruth 1:14). The millions who went back from the brink of Canaan did not write the next chapter of Bible history, but Joshua and Caleb did.

> *Back is never better. History is not kind to people who go back.*

Blessed Are the Complainers, for They Shall See Change

It's the complainers in all walks of life who are getting results. Thousands of lobbying groups, many of them small in number, refuse to be silent about their causes, whether it is

saving the whales, protecting the environ-
ment, or having better working conditions.
Celebrity TV chef Jamie Oliver recently took
on the British government about the poor
nutritional quality of school meals. His complaint was that children were being fed junk
food at the most formative time of their physical and intellectual development. His outrage
exposed the disgrace on national TV, and the
public protest he provoked resulted in a
change in the level of government funding for
school meals in just a matter of weeks. Many
before him had expressed a concern about
school meals, but a concern is not a complaint. A complaint fuels a vision to bring
change, and the consistent voice it becomes
makes real change possible.

Please understand that complaining is not
whining! Whiners are people who complain
about things that they permit and tolerate.
Whiners are a dime a dozen, but people with
a genuine complaint, who are willing to
become a force for change, are much rarer.

What Is Your Complaint?

What's your problem? What's your issue?
What can't you stand? What won't you put

up with? What do you have an attitude about? What bothers you about the church? What keeps you awake at night? What drives you crazy and gets you up on your "soap box" thumping the table in protest? Here you will find your life's cause and calling. Your irritation is your ministry. What you can't stand is what you were put here to stand up for.

Like Nehemiah, I can't stand the broken-down state that much of the church is in today. Our testimony is in tatters, wc are the subject of reproach, have a reputation for irrele-

Your irritation is your ministry. What you can't stand is what you were put here to stand up for.

vance and arrogance, and lack credibility. Much of the church, like Nehemiah's wall, is broken down, dysfunctional, and in urgent need of restoration. It angers me to see how secular TV portrays the "pompous preacher" as the stereotypical church leader. It angers me that no one turns to the church for wisdom on the serious issues of life. It angers me that every Sunday millions are shopping in superstores and malls and only a few are in church. But I can't blame them for choosing the mall instead of church because at least they go home with something they want or need. Sadly, that is not the case in many churches, and the churches should offer what people want and need.

170 Complaints

In our church we currently have about 170 ministries. We list all of them in our Directory of Ministries—a tool to help new people discover what's going on and to help everyone find their niche in ministry. This directory should really be called a "Directory of Complaints" because every ministry is actually someone's complaint. The vast majority of these ministries were started by church members who, since our crossing over, have flourished in the people-empowering culture we created. We on the pastoral staff refused to become the champions of causes we didn't feel were ours, so we created a culture that says, "If you're angry about it, fix it!"

People have complaints about training, music, kids' church, youth, security, visitor experience, tidiness, catering and hospitality, media, marriage, money management, transport, poverty, homelessness, prostitution, drug addiction, housing, care of the elderly, folks who are in prison, and so on. The people leading these ministries are doing so because they have an irritation about it. Their vision of what they can do is coming from their complaint about what was once done poorly or, worse than that, never done at all.

If something bothers you, if you feel something should be done, that someone should say something, that someone should stand up and stand out, then don't just go and tell your leaders. Do something. You're noticing it for a reason; you feel strongly about it for a reason. And the reason is, it's your complaint, which is the beginning of your vision. In the same place that you find your life's complaint you will find your life's call. So, be careful what you complain about because you just may start a ministry!

People inevitably come and go from these various ministries in our church because time and commitment separates the helpers of the vision from the carriers of the cause that birthed it. But true leaders are always carriers, not just helpers.

Choose Your Complaint; Choose Your Enemies

The great thing about identifying and then choosing your complaint is that it enables you to choose your own enemies. I've spent years of my ministry fighting for things that I didn't really care about, but those over me did. I defended various rules and church practices that my leadership felt were fundamental, but hand on heart, I disagreed. If you spend your life fighting someone else's enemies, you will ultimately violate yourself. Your soul begins to resent taking mental and emotional beatings for what it knows your heart doesn't really care about.

I wept over people leaving our church, when in my heart I was glad to see the back of them. I separated from some over tithing, authority, and the role of Ephesians 4 Ministries, when I knew these things were not important enough to lose people over.

If you keep asking your body and soul to hand you the physical and emotional strength to fight a war your heart is not in, they will eventually shut down on you. Alternatively if your body and soul know that this is something you would genuinely die for, they will fight with you and hand you the resources you need for as long as it takes, without ever leading a mutiny against you. You can be at war every day for

You can be at war every day for a cause you adore and still sleep like a baby, be happy, and keep your joy.

a cause you adore and still sleep like a baby, be happy, and keep your joy. How? By making sure that the war you're in is tied to the fundamental complaint of your life. Those who don't share your complaint will never understand you. Those who do understand will never forgive you for walking away from a fight that you were put on the planet to win. Winning your war is always about others, often thousands and millions of others, who need you to sustain your complaint until the vision becomes their reality too.

Making the Vision Plain for Runners

God told Habakkuk to make the vision plain and give it to runners. Making a vision plain is easy when your complaint is clear. Making a vision plain is not just about what I see, but what I feel about what I see. I don't just want you to see what I see, but I want you to feel what I feel. What makes people want to run with a vision isn't intellectual, it's emotional, and your complaint provides the emotional energy you need to inspire other runners.

Sadly, many pulpits are filled with intellect but are devoid of emotion. Passion rules the universe. Without passion nobody becomes a runner. Effective communication is 20 percent what you know and 80 percent how you feel about what you know. Where this ratio is reversed, passionate people are viewed as odd or highly strung and told to calm down and chill out. But the last thing you need to do is calm down! Don't ever try to calm down about things you feel deeply passionate about; those things have to do with your destiny.

Don't ever try to calm down about things you feel deeply passionate about; those things have to do with your destiny.

Runners

Pastors frequently ask me how I get people to run with the vision, so they can understand how to get people to run with theirs. My answer always includes an explanation that it is not our job to "get people to run with our vision." Our job is simply to communicate our vision effectively. Then, who runs may be a shock to us! I found that during our "crossing over" as a church, many of my so-called leaders didn't move, but many others took off like sprinters from the blocks, heralding the vision because they shared the complaint.

There's a runner for every vision and a vision for every runner. God is in the business of matching runners with vision.

Everybody should be running, but not everybody runs the same. People need to find their race, find their distance and style. In the church some will be sprinters with an ability to move fast in the early stages of a vision. Others will be hurdlers who are built for overcoming problems. Some will be marathon runners who can stick with a thing for years without wavering. Many projects fail because we entrust them to the wrong kind of runners. Don't put short attention span sprinters in charge of marathon projects. Don't ask people to start up a project if they're not good under the starter gun. Don't ask people to troubleshoot and problem solve if they're not gifted at jumping hurdles. There are runners for every aspect of the vision. What kind of runner are you?

To every leader reading this, stop trying

Stop trying to give the vision to sitters, sleepers, and vision tasters. Give the vision to runners.

to give the vision to sitters, sleepers, and vision tasters. Give the vision to runners who are simply complainers with a vision of how to fix things. Keep running toward that vision and never lose touch with the complaint that fueled it, because without a complaint your vision will perish.

Chapter 12

Live Full but Die Empty

I have thought long and hard about this final chapter and what I want to leave with you as my closing words. I've decided to ask you to think about how you want to die, about how you want to finish. What legacy do you want to leave to the next generation? I've decided to ask you to live full. But please, whatever you do, die empty!

Elisha's Bones

> Elisha died and was buried. Now Moabite raiders used to enter the

> country every spring. Once while
> some Israelites were burying a man,
> suddenly they saw a band of raiders;
> so they threw the man's body into
> Elisha's tomb. When the body touched
> Elisha's bones, the man came to life
> and stood up on his feet (2 Kings
> 13:20–21 NIV).

What an amazing story, but why is it even in the Bible? This story has no context to it; it's a kind of postscript footnote at the end of Elisha's life. It's not a story about those who were burying their friend, nor is it a story about what happened to the man after he raised from the dead. It doesn't explain itself; it lacks a point; it draws us in but leaves us wondering what we were intended to see. The whole episode sits awkwardly in 2 Kings, yet God included it for a reason. It was in pursuit of this reason that my mind and heart inquired, and my conclusion will close this book.

The mystery of this story is hidden inside those old dead bones of Elisha. Locked up and lying dormant for years within those bones was a residue of unused power—and what power! The power was able to blast a dead man back into the land of the living by merely touching them. For all those years since Elisha had died and his body had decayed, a miracle-working power was dormant in his remains. Though Elisha had left the planet, his power hadn't. But why? For some reason Elisha died incomplete; he lived full, but he didn't die empty—he died with unspent power still stored within him. Why would all this power be locked up in that tomb and wasted in those buried bones? What's the point? What possible good could it do anyone?

This story has become a fundamental guiding principle for my life: what God gives us to be spent on the earth must stay on the earth. We can't take it with us; heaven doesn't need it, and God doesn't want it back. We must die empty, fully spent, with nothing held back, nothing in reserve, nothing we wish we had done, and no one we wish we had helped. We are supposed to start full and finish empty, and what we leave in the tank is what was intended to help someone whom we never got around to helping.

> What God gives us to be spent on the earth must stay on the earth. We can't take it with us; heaven doesn't need it, and God doesn't want it back.

If someone gives you a gift certificate to be spent in a certain store, you can't spend it in another; the voucher comes with rules and limitations. The same is true of our lives and the treasure God has placed within them. The voucher of our life has "planet earth" stamped all over it; you can't spend it in heaven, it's the wrong store. You can't spend what was intended for lost people in the church; it's still the wrong store. We are blessed to be a blessing, or in other words, we are filled to get empty.

I have determined that when I enter heaven, I will be empty. Nothing I didn't say, nothing I didn't do, no one I didn't help, and nowhere I wanted to go will remain. I want to die with an empty bank account, or at least with any remaining money earmarked and on its way to where it should go. I refuse to die with the secret recipe, with things I didn't pass on because I enjoyed having them to myself. I refuse to die alone without spiritual sons and daughters into whom my life has been poured and who will continue to live. I refuse to die grasping a baton that I should have passed years ago.

We must live to get empty, not to stay full, and when we die our bones must be just bones, not capsules containing someone's miracle. I wonder how much power is locked up inside the church, how many people's miracles are on hold because they are stuck in a storage container called the church.

I really think that Elisha, in the closing moments of his life, tried to empty himself into King Jehoash. Years earlier he had tried to empty himself into his servant Gehazi, but clearly Gehazi's heart wasn't right and Elisha's anointing couldn't penetrate that vessel. King Jehoash was not a spiritual man so he was a poor candidate for Elisha's power to be poured into. Nevertheless, on his deathbed Elisha sent for the king, and the Bible records one of the saddest and most tragic encounters ever to take place between a prophet and a king:

I wonder how much power is locked up inside the church, how many people's miracles are on hold because they are stuck in a storage container called the church.

Now Elisha was suffering from the illness from which he died. Jehoash king of Israel went down to see him and wept over him. "My father! My father!" he cried. "The chariots and horsemen of Israel!" Elisha said, "Get a bow and some arrows," and he did so. "Take the bow in your hands," he said to the king of Israel. When he had taken it, Elisha put his hands on the king's hands. "Open the east window," he said, and he opened it. "Shoot!"

Elisha said, and he shot. "The LORD's arrow of victory, the arrow of victory over Aram!" Elisha declared. "You will completely destroy the Arameans at Aphek." Then he said, "Take the arrows," and the king took them. Elisha told him, "Strike the ground." He struck it three times and stopped. The man of God was angry with him and said, "You should have struck the ground five or six times; then you would have defeated Aram and completely destroyed it. But now you will defeat it only three times." Elisha died and was buried.

Now Moabite raiders used to enter the country every spring.

Once while some Israelites were burying a man, suddenly they saw a band of raiders; so they threw the man's body into Elisha's tomb. When the body touched Elisha's bones, the man came to life and stood up on his feet (2 Kings 13:14–21 NIV).

What a tragedy! The king didn't have a clue what was going on, and Elisha knew that the deadline for his unspent powers was about to expire. The frustration in Elisha's heart in this deathbed scene is palpable; surrounded by fools who had no inkling about his desperation to offload his excess anointing must have been pure agony for Elisha.

Don't leave your handoff so late; start looking now for those who will be with you at the end of your life. The handoff is always in place before the race even begins.

Start looking now for those who will be with you at the end of your life. The handoff is always in place before the race even begins.

At the end of the apostle Paul's life he already had young Timothy in place to carry on his work. He writes to this young disciple, *For I am already being poured out like a drink offering, and the time has come for my departure. I have fought the good fight, I have finished the race, I have kept the faith* (2 Timothy 4:6–7 NIV).

The Ultimate Dying Empty Scene

Paul died empty, bone-dry, and so should you. Christ's death on the cross was the ultimate "dying empty" scene. In His final moments of life and in utter agony, Jesus reached out to the thief on the cross beside Him telling him, *Today you will be with me in paradise* (Luke 23:43 NIV).

> Christ's death on the cross was the ultimate "dying empty" scene.

It was as if He knew that He still wasn't empty, that He still held someone's miracle within Him, and that someone was a thief who was scheduled to die on the same day. See Him also reaching out from the cross to take care of His heartbroken, devastated mother. He looks down at her and with His dying breath charges John with responsibility for caring for His mother: *When Jesus saw his mother there, and the disciple whom he loved standing nearby, he said to his mother, "Dear woman, here is your son," and to the disciple, "Here is your mother." From that time on, this disciple took her into his home* (John 19:26–27 NIV).

On the cross Jesus even asked for a small drink. But the Gospel of John tells us He only did this to fulfill an Old Testament Scripture which foretold that He would do it (John 19:28–29). When Jesus had completed this final act, He said, *It is finished,* bowed His head, and dismissed His spirit (John 19:30). That's what I call dying empty—totally empty!

What we don't do or say, win or fight for, our children will be left to deal with. Throughout my life and twenty-five years in ministry, I have at times had the overwhelming sense that some of the battles I have fought were never mine in the first place. Some of the things I have wrestled with had a kind of familiarity to them as if they had been around a long time. Every Goliath we don't kill will live to terrorize our children and their children. I don't want to leave them to fight my giants. Many of

Every Goliath we don't kill will live to terrorize our children and their children.

the things I have had to confront and remove from the church have been the result of my forefathers not dying empty and leaving me with their unfinished business.

Now, having crossed our church over, we are living in the Promised Land I first saw all those years ago. We are a church that is drawn to the emptiness in our city and world, and a church that is determined to live full but die empty. I pray with all my heart that something of our journey will be helpful to you, that you will help me to die empty by allowing me to pour some of my life into yours. This book may well be the defining book of my life and ministry, and if it is, then the most important work of my life is to help others in their crossing over experiences. It is to that end that I have written this book and to that end I now pray.

Epilogue: A Prayer

Father, take my life and use it to help others. Lord, I know that what I have lived through these past years was not just about me but also about Your church across the earth. By Your grace I am a survivor, and I will tell others. God, I pray that this book may become a lifeline and a weapon for dominion to all who have set their hearts on the pilgrimage called crossing over.

I also pray that this book will be an endless cause of irritation to every demon assigned by hell to sedate and put to sleep the church of Jesus Christ across the earth. Awake! Awake, O Zion! Come clothe yourself with strength. This is our time and our turn. Let's make heaven breathless and hell speechless!

More information about the ministry of
Pastor Paul Scanlon and the Abundant Life
Church, Bradford, can be obtained from:

Abundant Life Church
Wapping Road
Bradford
BD3 0EQ
England

Tel: +44 (0)1274 307233

Or visit the website: www.alm.org.uk